BETTY WHITE
IN PERSON

BETTY WHITE IN PERSON

Betty White

Doubleday
New York
1987

DESIGNED BY PETER R. KRUZAN

Library of Congress Cataloging-in-Publication Data

White, Betty, 1924–
Betty White in person.

1. White, Betty, 1924–   .   2. Television actors and
actresses—United States—Biography.   I. Title.
PN2287.W4577A3   1987   814′.54   87-13265
ISBN: 0-385-23916-5

For Tess,
Superfriend I

Acknowledgments

To Bart Andrews and Sherry Robb, my agents, for making me say yes to the project in the beginning; To Loretta Barrett, my editor, for all her help . . . especially her invaluable positive response, each time I needed it most; To Gail Clark, without whom I couldn't keep my life in working order, let alone write a book; To Rudy Behlmer for his patience, understanding, and encouragement; To Kay Daly and to Lee Moorer for their unfailing love and support and "being there" through all the years . . . upon which I depend so much; To Aimée Friedman for her unmeasured honesty and enthusiasm; To Mary Ellen and Ed Hicks for picking up the pieces; To all the friends and Superfriends, past and present, who have made weaving the tapestry such an interesting game for me.

As well as to Timothy, Cricket, and T.K. for their constant presence and comfort throughout this adventure;
My deepest thanks

Contents

Foreword

This book turned into something completely different from what was originally intended . . . not better . . . just different. I don't really know at just what point I lost control.

There was a meeting . . . I remember that . . . and I went in fully intending to say a polite but definite no to writing another book. I recall someone explaining, gently, that all it would be was a series of short essays on a variety of subjects from my frame of reference.

Oh! Well! *That* was different! It didn't really matter that I hadn't the foggiest as to what that meant . . . it sounded great in the meeting. It was not five minutes after I arrived before I was nodding like a Christmas tiger . . . "Oh, yes! That sounds like it would be fun to do!"

The backbone of an earthworm.

Having been a dedicated closet writer . . . we are legion . . . I have been jotting down thoughts and ideas for as long as I can remember. Not for anyone to see . . . it was my own private little exercise. It also helped remind me of things that might otherwise be erased from the mental tape recorder.

So that is what I assumed I would be working on . . . random observations . . . nothing personal.

What I soon discovered in the course of this adventure

is that there is no way to report on your feelings and
opinions *without* getting personal. It is impossible to
avoid the "I, me, and my" syndrome. This immediately
steers you off course, away from any objectivity whatsoever . . . and you find yourself smack in the middle of
the Sea of Subjection.

That is how this whole thing got away from me, and
took on a life of its own.

As a result, you are going to hear a great deal about the
people who have been closest to me . . . Allen Ludden
. . . my mother and father . . . the people I work with
. . . my friends . . . and Superfriends.

You will hear about what makes me laugh . . . and
what makes me cry . . . what I love . . . and what I
hate.

What you will *not* hear is "a series of short essays on a
variety of subjects from my frame of reference."

Sorry. It just didn't come out that way.

I

OFF THE TOP OF MY HEAD

On Titles

Choosing a name for anything is difficult. Yet, it is so important to choose the one that fits . . . whether it's a baby . . . or a pet . . . or even a book. There are so many choices . . .

At first, they wanted to call this book *Betty White's Golden Rules.*

Is that not the worst title you ever heard? Talk about a turnoff. Believe me, it wasn't my idea. It was probably a committee decision . . . putting the quote celebrity unquote name in the title, plus throwing in the word "golden" as a subtle reminder of a certain television show, in case the quote celebrity unquote name doesn't ring a bell.

In any event, I wasn't about to tell anybody I hated the title. That would be impolite . . . and besides, they might take back their suggestion for me to do a book. So I said, "Swell."

Titles have always given me a problem. There are so many good ones, I was never able to narrow it down to one.

This was not a major problem until I was about eight, and started my first book. It was a compilation of short . . . very . . . pieces about animals I had known . . .

or seen. A half page on a moose glimpsed in a meadow as
we drove by . . . two pages on several bears in Yellow-
stone National Park . . . and another three pages on
my own pets, past and present. Of course, I wrote bigger
then, so the page count is unreliable. Unfortunately, the
book struck a snag when I couldn't decide between two
great titles . . . *My Petography* . . . or *My Animalography.*
For this reason, plus a rather weak plot, the project just
never got off the ground.

When I was eleven, I wrote my first *serious* piece of any
length . . . 107 pages, handwritten . . . in ink! I
found it recently in an old suitcase. It was a Western
story, about a girl and her dying brother. After his death
(page 4), our heroine moved to Wyoming, to a "vast
ranch" that her uncle had conveniently left her at some
time or other. There, she had numerous adventures with
horse thieves, a hero named Montana (not necessarily in
that order) . . . and the inevitable puppy, Rustie.

This opus, I suspect, might have run on longer than
the 107 pages . . . but there must have been a deadline
involved in some way . . . because on page 106, our
girl suddenly woke up . . . found her brother, not only
alive, but *recovering* . . . and the whole Wyoming experience had been . . . what else? . . . a dream.

With a grabber like that, the right title is mandatory.

I had *two* that were equally powerful . . . I wound up
using both of them.

SOCIETY OR COWGIRL?
or
FROM DEBUT TO ROUNDUP

I mean, what would *you* have done?

My father and my uncle really liked it . . . not so
much the plot as the writing. You see, I had just learned
the parts of speech at school and, not wanting to be
redundant, I never had anyone just *say* anything. They
queried, or retorted . . . "Oh, that's not true!" she in-
terjected. "Oh, yes, it is!" he ejaculated.

It wasn't until years later that I learned *why* my father
and my uncle liked it so much.

That could account for my excessive use of exclama-
tion marks!

Once we got past the *Golden Rules* business . . . (if
you want those, you've picked up the wrong book) . . .
I suggested *Betty White: On and On.* That, it seemed, had a
nice double intent . . . Betty has been around a long
time in television . . . plus the fact that all the pieces
herein start with "on." Not bad, I thought. Some wiser
head pointed out that that could be an open invitation to
a critic . . ." She certainly does . . . Betty White does
go———"

How about *Betty White's Short Pieces?* No, no . . . So I
said, "Let them work out the title. I wash my hands of it."

No sooner said than they did just that . . . they came
up with a title I liked a lot. For indeed, this is Betty White
. . . in person.

On Names

Having such a problem with titles . . . what if I had had to choose a "stage name"?! My career would have been over before I could have made up my mind what to call myself!

My folks solved that for me. I was christened Betty Marion White. Not Elizabeth . . . Betty. They didn't want any of the derivatives to sneak in . . . Liz, Lizzie, Liza, Beth. So, to leave no room for doubt, it was Betty.

Twice on stage, I was Elizabeth. Once, when we did *Pride and Prejudice* as our senior play at Beverly Hills High School. I played Elizabeth . . . we figured Jane Austen would have taken a dim view if we'd called the character Betty. Then again, in 1950, with my first television series . . . on live in Los Angeles until we syndicated in 1953. The creator of that series, George Tibbles, called it "Life with Elizabeth." Except for those two lapses, it's been plain old Betty . . . (in those days, the old was figurative.)

Even as simple a name as Betty soon developed a nickname, and, ironically, it was my mother who started calling me Bets. For years it stuck among my friends . . . with some, even today. But the men in my life . . . romantically . . . never called me that. Perhaps because my mother did.

When I married years ago, my husband's name was Lane Allan . . . however, that was his professional name. Legally, he was Albert Wooten, so I wound up with *three* names to remember . . . Mrs. Lane Allan, Mrs. Albert Wooten, and/or Betty White. At the time of our divorce, I took my own name back, and isn't it a good thing I did? When I married Allen, I could have wound up Betty Allan Ludden! Lane was a casting director for Universal Studios, and years later . . . long after Allen and I were married . . . Lane cast me in a role in "Lucas Tanner," a series David Hartman was doing at the time. Lane and I were friends as well as exes, so one day Allen Ludden, Lane Allan, and Betty White Wooten Allan Ludden all had lunch together in the commissary at Universal. It was a good time, and I was very proud of both these fine men. I would love to be very sophisticated and say, "Why not! That's the way things are done!" It is . . . I guess, or should be . . . but I will admit, way deep down, it felt a little strange. I wonder if it did for them?

Every once in a while on "The Golden Girls," Blanche rattles off a slew of Southern double and triple names . . . Billy Bob . . . Bobby Jo Sue . . . whatever. Sometimes they come right out of her Oklahoma background . . . and how I love it when she starts reminiscing about back home. Not on camera . . . in real life!

On rehearsal days, periodically we will have a short

break, and often the four of us just stay in the set and
chat until we start up again. Well . . . every so often, we
stop short, look at each other, and break up. Somebody
. . . usually Bea . . . will say, "My God, we sound just
like 'The Golden Girls'!"

Rue was christened Eddie Rue McClanahan . . .
which came from a combination of Rhue-Nell, her mother's name, and her dad's, William Edwin. That's a pretty
good fistful for an autograph . . . Rue McClanahan.

Because Betty White was such a simple name (no
cracks) the obvious question was always "Is that your real
name?" My stock answer was always "Wouldn't I have
made up something a little more exciting?"

In truth, not really . . . not at that point in time.
When I started out, ordinary names with ordinary spell-
ing were par for the course. Lucille Fay Le Sueur became
Joan Crawford. Frances Gumm turned into Judy Garland
. . . The same was true of the men . . . Spangler Ar-
lington Brugh distilled down to Robert Taylor, and, of
course, Archie Leach was immediately changed to Cary
Grant.

Not too long after that, we went through a period
where the fellows were given macho-sounding one-sylla-
ble names . . . Rock! Tab! Touch!

Okay, now fast forward up to the present. Almost anything works. Cher. No fat on that name! If you'd like
something a bit longer, try Mary Elizabeth Mastrantonio.
Ask *her* for an autograph and you could be going steady
before she finished signing her name. She'll never have a
racehorse named after her . . . I think they're only allowed seventeen letters.

Some of today's star names are not only long, but unusual . . . often triple or hyphenated, or both, and the spelling is exotic, to say the least.

Let's take "The Cosby Show," just as a for instance:

Aside from the star, himself, we have Phylicia Rashad, who, when the show started, was Phylicia Ayers-Allen. Keshia Knight Pulliam. Tempestt Bledsoe. Lisa Bonet. Malcolm-Jamal Warner.

Obviously, *that* show will never work . . . with names like that no one will ever be able to remember who's in it!!

It goes to show that no matter what you call it, if you've got it, you've got it. Their signed cast picture must be poster size.

On thinking it over, signing Rue McClanahan is a snap.

But, Betty Wooten-Allan White-Ludden still sounds a little much.

On People Watching

Ever looked up into a clear blue sky and followed a contrail to its source . . . a tiny speck that you know is a jetliner?

It never fails to intrigue me . . . realizing that inside that tiny speck there are people eating, drinking, working, dozing. For a few hours that speck is their world.

It is true that the same principle applies to a drop of water, or a grain of sand . . . but this is different. We *know* those people. We've *been* those people. As a rule, of course, when we are up there we are all so variously occupied, only rarely do we take time to throw a curious glance out the window at those on the ground.

Traveling alone affords a wonderful opportunity to observe people from a completely detached point of view, and can be a great learning experience.

How people *look* is the least of it . . . the behavior patterns are what you recognize. Those attached as pairs or groups can quickly be sorted into the ones who like each other, as opposed to those who are merely resigned. Lone passengers also fall into two main categories . . . the talkers, and the ones who yearn to be left to their own devices.

The Talker is easy to spot. He is ready with a cheery self-introduction and opening gambit even before the door is closed. He would prefer sitting next to a Passive Listener, but should he draw another Talker it's all right, because they won't be listening to each other anyhow. His frustration is apparent, however, if he is unfortunate enough to get a seat partner who immediately dives into book or briefcase . . . these individuals are often tough to break down. He bides his time until the food is served . . . and just as the book or work is set aside momentarily . . . he makes another assault. If his opponent is quick enough to go for the earphones, Talker is finally forced to concede.

Perhaps someday there will be seating arrangements that can be reserved ahead, designating seat partner type preference . . . much like the smoking and nonsmoking sections today.

Being a confirmed book/briefcase type, I must still admit, reluctantly, that I have had some memorable conversations in the air. On two occasions they were so interesting that I jotted down notes afterward, which I still have. And the best exception of all, a dear friend whom I cherish, is someone my mother met on a flight from New York to Los Angeles. Mom and Aimée Friedman struck up a conversation that lasted three thousand miles and twenty years.

Before I abandon my book and briefcase entirely, though, it pays to remember that those gems are but tiny islands in a sea of inconsequential small talk. Overall, observing is still more fun in this situation, I find, than participating . . . and it can become a real spectator sport during the occasional post-cocktail-hour mating dance!

An airliner is just one small arena for people watchers. It not only works anywhere, but there are so many variations on the game.

One day on Wilshire Boulevard in Beverly Hills, I saw a motorcycle policeman writing out a ticket at the curb. Not too unusual . . . except that it was a very tall policeman, and the tiniest, lowest little red sports car I ever saw. What made the moment memorable . . . the cop was literally down on both knees on the street in order to talk to the driver.

People *listening* is also fun when you're by yourself. Riding up an escalator at Lord & Taylor, I once over-

heard two women talking behind me . . . and the scrap
of conversation was brief, but vivid. All I heard was one
woman say, "We adored Rome, but I spent so much
money! Even on the way to the airport, I had to stop at
one more gallery. I paid a bundle for this old master-
piece, and when I got it on the plane the goddam thing
was still wet!"

Judging from my own cluttered mind, I know that it is
possible, on different levels, to be thinking of three unrelated things, while outwardly we appear to be doing
something else entirely. It's sometimes interesting to try
and surmise what is *really* going on in someone else's
head. Certain clues can be helpful . . . facial expression, body language, tone of voice . . . from which you
make up a whole scenario to suit your own imagination.
Of course, there is no way of knowing if you were even
close, but you've had fun guessing.

If anyone was ever able to take a look inside my head,
they'd get the net.

Yet *another* variation on observing people is also good
mental gymnastics, and can be a welcome diversion if
you are stuck in a waiting situation. Glance at someone
for a split second, then look away and see how many
details about that individual you can recall. Then you can
look again and check your description. Not so easy, is it?
But you'll find you do get better at this with practice. Just
be sure to keep your glances subtle . . . don't get so
carried away that you forget they *could* be looking back at
you.

And sometimes they are.

When someone has been appearing on television for a hundred years, as I have, it is only to be expected that people may recognize you. Television, more than any other medium, invites informality . . . which I think is great. At the market, for example, people go by and say, "Hi, Betty" in passing . . . as you would to anyone who has been visiting your house for years. Movie stars, on the other hand, seem to have something of an invisible shield around them. Onscreen they are larger than life, so it follows they might be somewhat more intimidating in person.

Whatever the reason for a "celebrity" identity, it does tend to inhibit your own people watching, because you are no longer anonymous . . . to some degree you are "on." But it is still fun to watch the different ways people handle the situation.

For the most part, the folks who come up to you are warm and polite . . . sometimes even apologetic. They say something generous then move on. Now and then there is the accuser . . . "You're Betty White, aren't you? I knew it!" You feel so guilty suddenly, you are forced to confess. "Yes . . . I am. I'm sorry!"

Then there are the ones who seem to think you can neither see nor hear. They nudge the person next to them and point. "Look! I told you that's her! She's not as fat as I thought she was!" The fact that they are standing three feet from you doesn't faze them an iota . . . they are so used to talking in front of their TV set.

It always amazes me how readily they can spot you . . . no matter how you may look. Especially little kids. I can have a scarf on my hair, be wearing glasses, and

bundled up to here in a raincoat . . . not for disguise,
but for weather . . . and, sure enough . . . "Hi, Betty!
I recognized your voice right off!"

Far from resenting the familiarity, I think it is a lovely
vote of confidence. Ninety-nine percent of the time the
greetings are graciously enthusiastic . . . and brief. I
am very flattered.

Whether one is the watcher or the watchee . . . people are entertaining.

On Awareness

If there was such a thing as an "awareness meter," people watchers should score well, wouldn't you think? Not
always.

First, some ground rules must be established as to
what constitutes awareness, which probably varies with
each individual. It is also difficult . . . if not impossible
. . . to measure. Some people can be very conscious of
things around them, yet keep still about it. Others of us
seem to have a compulsion to belabor the obvious with
comment.

I plead guilty to the latter, but it is not intentional, so
help me . . . it just pops out. It doesn't necessarily
make me a bad person, but I have a maddening habit of
interrupting myself to say, "Look at that sky!" (or whatever) . . . and then going right on with the conversa-

tion. I *know* it is maddening, because a close friend, who has known me forever, uses it as a sarcastic putdown whenever he wants to get my goat. He contends that he has seen whatever I am pointing out, but doesn't find it remarkable. Heaven *forfend* he should waste a remark!

Naturally, I will take his word that he noticed whatever it was . . . even if he was looking the other way. But what he never will understand is that I wasn't pointing it out for his benefit . . . only for my own. An involuntary gasp of appreciation, I guess.

So "Look at that sky!" has become a cliché between us that can apply to almost anything. He has known me for so many years, of course, . . . he thinks cliché is my second language.

The awareness that I find appealing in people is really nothing more than sensitivity, and it is certainly not limited to scenery alone.

Someone can be *aware* . . . that a person is being ignored in a group. How many times have you seen people get so engrossed in a conversation that they keep shifting positions, until one poor guy finds himself looking at nothing but backs? This isn't deliberate rudeness . . . just insensitivity.

Someone can be *aware* . . . that there are others trying to see what he is looking at, and he will make a little room accordingly.

Someone can be *aware* . . . that a car is waiting for her parking place, so she will postpone touching up her lipstick until later.

And like that.

Sometimes it is difficult for me to believe that people

aren't acting out of sheer malice. It seems inconceivable, with all the bodies on this planet, that anyone could fail to notice all those others besides himself. But . . . amazingly . . . that's the way it is.

Perhaps it is a form of subliminal self-preservation . . . insulation against the burgeoning density of the population. Survival of the fittest . . . or the most insensitive.

Whatever excuses we find for them, I hate to think the inconsiderate shall inherit the earth. In order to survive it is not really mandatory to carry on a conversation at full voice in a movie theater!

I am beginning to get testy, which serves no purpose. Let's go back to where we came in . . . we were talking about being observant.

Noticing something different about someone can be flattering. Or at least preferable to not noticing at all. The other day at work, a fellow I know said that it took his wife a week to realize he had shaved off the mustache he'd worn for fifteen years. Maybe she just didn't find it "remarkable."

Being aware of a change in the sound of your car's engine . . . if you discover it early enough . . . may save a repair bill down the road. (This one I flunk out on completely.)

Any Californian venturing east of the Rocky Mountains is sure to be bombarded with "Don't you miss the change of seasons?" This is a question I can understand because, as has been indicated, I speak fluent cliché.

Well, to the observer who is *seeing* . . . not just looking . . . we *have* changes in the seasons, even in crazy
old California. We just go about it more subtly. Our
leaves turn in the fall without being ostentatious about it.
We know when it's winter because we cut our roses back
so we will have gorgeous blooms again in twenty minutes. We also know it's winter when the wind blows chill
through our California bungalows, even though all the
doors and windows are closed and the air conditioning is
off.

Spring is a little harder to detect, since everything has
been in bloom all winter . . . but a sure sign is when the
mockingbirds sing all night, and the hills turn from gold
to green. Easterners call our winter hills brown . . . we
know they are gold.

Summer is the most obvious of all, since it is brushfire
season, and it's not easy to be subtle about that.

It doesn't matter *where* you live if you are a sky watcher
. . . the sky is great everywhere. Clouds are never the
same, but always a spur to the imagination. If you see one
spectacular sunset, you have *not* seen them all.

And then there is the moon! It has been doing its
number, month in and month out, for quite some time,
but it is still a constant source of wonder and beauty to
the romantics of this world. On moonlit nights I make it a
point to take one last look before I go to bed . . . in
case one or the other of us may not be there tomorrow
night. How must those men feel who have *walked* there!?

Some people just don't know . . . or care . . . what
they're missing.

But then . . . think of all the things they see that I
miss.

"Look at that sky!"

"What sky?"

On Animals . . . Naturally

It is difficult for me to stay off the subject of animals at
any time . . . but well nigh impossible when we are talking about awareness. Animals *invented* it . . . they survive by it . . . and, since moving in to live with us humans, have perfected it to a fine art.

Our pets are tuned in to us at all times, and remember-
ing this, we can begin to appreciate the wordless communication that exists between us and our dog or cat. The
longer we live together, the more mutually perceptive we
become. This same rapport is a little harder to come by
with people . . . words get in the way, and basic meaning or intent becomes clouded. Not so with the four-
legged creatures that share our lives. They keep it simple
. . . dogs in particular. Cats are every bit as sensitive,
but much more sophisticated. They are willing to pretend to cool it until there is some reason to get involved.
With dogs . . . every moment is deemed worthy of
their complete attention.

A dog can be sound asleep, but so much as tiptoe to
another chair . . . the ears lift, the eyebrows twitch,

and, usually, the head comes up momentarily until you settle again.

The best wordless communicator I've known was our Sooner . . . a golden retriever/Labrador (at the very least) mix that we found on the street one night when he was only a few months old. After healing up a broken leg, we brought him home for fifteen wonderful years. Talk about being on the same wavelength! It got so that if I simply smiled at him across the room, he would wag his tail . . . but if I frowned, his ears would go down, and his eyebrows (trust me) became question marks! He didn't *always* do *exactly* as I wanted, but it wasn't ever because he didn't understand . . . and he knew I out-ranked him. Once I realized that he was as smart as I was, we got along fine.

My black cat, T.K., has another approach. She thinks she won't give me the satisfaction of letting me know she is listening, but again, it is her ears that are the dead giveaway. When I speak to her she can look the other way in an elaborate show of inattention, but those black ears are turning like radar scopes, taking in everything.

This constant two-way communication does keep a house from feeling empty. You *have* to pay attention to something besides your own concerns . . . maybe only subconsciously . . . whether you want to or not.

At long last, pets have been publicly recognized as first-rate therapists. They have been doing the job since time began, but it has only been in the last couple of decades that we caught on. For the ill, for the disturbed, the disabled, the disenfranchised . . . probably most of all for the elderly . . . pets can be a link with life.

My friend Tom Watson and I wrote a book, *Betty White's Pet Love,* on the subject of pets used in therapy. In the course of our research, we came across example after example in which animals established a contact, or triggered a response, where a human therapist could not. We didn't just read about it . . . we *saw* it. And these stories continue to come in almost daily.

Many in the medical community, doctors as well as nurses, who were disbelievers going in . . . have become avid converts after seeing how deeply an animal can reach patients in certain situations. What I find surprising is that often the contact will work, even though a patient may not have been particularly animal-oriented in the past.

Dogs and cats aren't the only animals in the miracle-working business. Horses have proven invaluable, both physically and emotionally, in helping children suffering from various crippling diseases. Therapeutic riding programs were developed in England years ago, and are now found all over this country as well as abroad.

The physical therapy necessary in treating crippled children is often painful, and certainly tedious. Those same movements in many cases can be achieved by taking the little one out of a wheelchair and placing him on a horse. Can you imagine what a far-reaching lift *that* is? The child who, until now, has only been looking up from a bed or a wheelchair is suddenly above it all . . . and, what's more, feels in charge of this huge animal beneath him.

The horse, too, seems to be fully aware of how important his passenger is, and behaves with appropriate care and patience.

One horse in particular I shall never forget. In Los Angeles there is a fine therapeutic riding program called "Ahead with Horses" under the direction of Liz Helms. One evening they had a demonstration for the public with some of the children involved in the program. They were a mixed group of assorted sizes and physical problems, but long on pride and enthusiasm.

The smallest was a boy no bigger than a *minute*, and the horse he rode looked enormous. A young gymnast (a volunteer with the group) walked beside, unobtrusively holding the child's belt for safety. I couldn't help noticing how tenderly the young man handled both the rider . . . and the horse. They proudly made their way around the ring, and when they had come full circle, the horse stopped and stood like a statue. The little one was lifted down, but instead of being put right into his chair, he was placed standing . . . with braces . . . on the ground. This tiny child reached toward the motionless horse and took three steps. It was one of those "moments."

Later the young man told me they were the first steps this little boy had taken . . . the added excitement of riding in the "show" had provided the little extra push that was needed to make it possible.

When I stroked the horse and told him how good *he* had been, too, the young fellow introduced us. "This is Promise Yourself." He grinned. "He's our best teacher. The kids can all relate to him because he's overcoming a problem, too. You see, he's blind."

On Measured Honesty

Could you make it through a whole day telling nothing but the truth? If you did, you might wind up losing some friends.

There are times when the absolute truth just won't cut it . . .

This certainly applies if you are in the acting business . . . where you are constantly obligated to make comment on the performances or productions of friends.

If it is a casual friendship, and the production is a bomb . . . you might try to make it through that minefield by being enthusiastically noncommittal. "Well, that was really something!" "*What* an evening!" But so many jokes have been made about that . . . "Well, you've done it again!" . . . that it's difficult to pull it off without sounding as though you are doing exactly what you are, in fact, doing.

Even dear close friends don't want to hear that a production is bad . . . yet they would be horrified if you lied to them. You must level to a certain extent . . . but if you really love them you don't have to go into chapter and verse about what a turkey it was. Merciful measured honesty.

There are so many instances when the *whole* truth can pose a problem.

Suppose someone I like is giving a party. What do I do? Make up a polite, if slightly creative excuse, or be truthful and say, "I don't like parties in general, and yours are the worst!" If I stopped with "I don't like parties in general," I *might* get by with it . . . but then I'd feel guilty, and worry . . . and . . . Well, I usually wind up going.

A friend of mine has what he considers to be the perfect solution. He simply says, "Sorry, I can't." No hemming or hawing, no embroidery . . . just "Sorry, I can't." And he leaves it at that. Maybe he is secure enough to get away with it, but with my luck they'd say, "Why not?"

Honesty is a virtue greatly to be admired, but it is strong medicine to be taken . . . and dished out . . . in careful doses. Being frank is fine, but not to the point of brutality. If you feel your "honest" opinion will really benefit someone, then go for it . . . but if the hurt incurred will outweigh the help, keep your mouth shut.

Truth is resilient and can be stretched pretty far. Lies . . . even little white ones . . . should be avoided like the plague . . . not only for moral reasons, but because, unless you are a master of the game (in which case, I don't want anything to do with you), they are almost always going to come back to haunt you. With a memory like mine, that goes without saying.

Where prevarication can really get you in trouble is in the early days of a relationship. In the euphoria of a new romance, you tend to enthuse and agree on things you might not like at all if you were in your right mind. Which, of course, you're not.

Be honest up front . . . for, should the relationship bloom into something more, you could find yourself going to hockey games for the rest of your life.

If, on the other hand, later on you finally have to own up to the fact that you were less than honest in the beginning, your credibility sustains a bruise. Even if it concerns something that seems too trivial to matter, it can start the mildew of doubt, and cause a problem when the big things come along.

And those big things do come along. That's when your honesty must be meted out very carefully. As a wise doctor I know put it, "You can call a spade a spade, but you don't have to call it a dirty old shovel." *Total* honesty can sometimes destroy hope in the other party. *Dis*honesty can destroy faith. It's a very fine line and there is no blueprint.

Keep the other person's well-being in mind when you feel an attack of soul-purging truth coming on. You may feel better for it, but you may have done some irreparable damage in the process.

Measured honesty is the best policy.

On Saving Things

At some time or other, everyone must feel a sense of drowning in a sea of things that are not quite throwawayable. At least I prefer to think I am not alone with this problem.

We all have different things that we save for a variety of reasons. Those reasons may say as much about us as that which we save.

It has been said that if you can organize your closet, you can organize your life. That could probably be stretched to include the garage as well . . . of course, the catch phrase is . . . *if* you can.

Many of us are of the "Waste Not, Want Not" persuasion, or the subspecies "This Will Come in Handy Someday." Consequently, valuable shelf space is taken up with coffee makers that no longer work, pieces of cardboard, plastic bubblewrap, extra accessories from a retired vacuum cleaner, and a myriad of florist's cheap glass flower vases. After the marginally fixable have been picked up by Goodwill, many of these things may still hang on through a couple of garage cleanings, but ultimately they will bite the dust . . . to make room for more.

The junk stuff is the easy part, and it will more or less take care of itself. A more difficult keepsake group to cope with is "Memorabilia." The subheadings on this category break down into "Nostalgia" and "Family Duty."

"Nostalgia" gets thinned out every so often by a relatively simple procedure . . . you deep-six something when you can no longer remember what it was saved to commemorate.

"Family Duty" gets more complicated. This consists of all those anonymous items you can't bring yourself to part with . . . not because you are attached to them, but . . . like the little brass camel box whose lid keeps falling off . . . they have been around for as long as you can remember. Eventually these may get packed away, but not actually disposed of . . . it has somehow become your "Family Duty" to perpetuate them.

However, *somebody* must have the courage to get rid of these things, judging by the number of quaint little shops proudly displaying these eyesores in their windows at astronomical prices. Keep anything long enough, as the old rule goes, and it will come back into fashion . . . becoming someone's treasured collector's item . . . no matter how ugly it may be.

Is it possible that I am not in the majority on this subject, after all? And another thought . . . even more disturbing . . . many of the things I have packed away originated from one source . . . a particularly unfavorite (a euphemism) aunt. Could it be that I have a latent fear that if I even considered getting rid of her things, she might come back to haunt me? Heaven forbid! She was bad enough the first time around.

Something else that just occurred to me . . . those shop windows I mentioned are always filled with old portraits and statuary . . . and to me *they all look like my aunt!* I may have stumbled on to the surface tip of a deep psychological iceberg here.

Let's get on safer ground that we can all share. For instance, isn't the tendency to clip things (or tear them) from newspapers and magazines fairly universal? "The sound of Sunday in our house," my husband used to say, "is the tearing of paper." Still is . . . articles, ads, recipes, photographs.

The photos I am always going to sketch or paint someday.

The recipes never get made, but they sound simple and wonderful.

The ads are obsolete before I get around to calling about them.

The articles *do* make it into the file, since I am sure I will want to refer to them at some future date. Obviously, on the rare occasion that that happens, I can never find the damned article.

My one point of pride is that I only tear from my own property. I consider myself a cut above those who mutilate the periodicals in doctors' offices or beauty shops. In those circumstances if something is absolutely irresistible, I will frantically try to scribble it down on whatever paper my purse contains. The result is not only illegible, but I am usually called away before I've finished copying. Once I did get a complete (short) recipe written down for grape pie, only to discover I had used the back of my parking ticket . . . which, of course, I had to give to the man in order to retrieve my car. I've tried to make the pie several times from memory, but I think I'm leaving something out. The only ingredients I remember for *sure* are the grapes.

Letters are something else that can gather and complicate your life. Other people always seem to save the right ones. They keep them in good order, then eventually publish them in a book for the historical benefit of the general public, or . . . if they contain some degree of prurient interest . . . personal profit. Even if they don't get published, such a collection will serve as a rich lode for some interested researcher of the future . . . (who, naturally, is writing a book.)

Unfortunately, the letters I have retained over the years have nothing to do with history or prurience . . . only sentimentality. By now, some of them have ceased to be anything more than familiar packages that, again, have been around long enough to earn a permanent place in the storage room. It's odd, but the letters I *wish* I had today are not to be found, although they were more important, even at the time, than the unnoteworthy notes that have survived. It could be that the special ones were carried with me until they fell apart.

At this late date it is unrealistic to believe I can change my ways. I will, no doubt, continue to save the worthless and discard the treasures. It will be up to the poor soul who has to sort it out after I'm gone to figure out what it all means. Good luck to whomever.

Of course, now I have roused my own curiosity to the extent that I may go back and read some of those old letters. There may be a book there.

II

ALL WORK
AND SOME PLAY

On Name-dropping

The fact that I have lived in or near Hollywood almost my entire life does not for one moment make me blasé about seeing celebrities in the flesh. (Figure of speech.)

Being able to count people who were once distant idols as close friends today still boggles my mind, and it's a privilege I will never take for granted. It absolutely knocks me out to come home and find a message that "Fred Astaire called."

This certainly doesn't mean that all my friends are showfolk . . . far from it. Some of my most cherished have no connection in any way. Nor does it mean that *all* the acquaintances who *are* in the business are simply swell. Some, you find yourself making excuses to avoid for one reason or another . . . just as in any slice of life.

What do entertainers do when they entertain each other? They talk shop a lot, admittedly . . . just as doctors talk medicine, teachers talk school, and lawyers talk your head off . . . but they are well informed and have varied interests on which they can hold forth with equal enthusiasm.

Some also play games.

Parties have never been my favorite pastime . . . Allen was the party boy . . . but there is one group I cannot resist. Burt Reynolds is more or less the ringleader, and usually winds up being host. The whole purpose of the evening is to play a game, similar to charades, only drawing on a blackboard instead of acting out. Sounds silly and harmless enough . . . but it gets even sillier than that, and we play for blood. Girls against the boys.

Over the years, the cast of characters has shifted slightly, but the nucleus remains pretty stable. (Anything but the appropriate word.) Along with Burt, of course, the group would include Mel Brooks and his wife, Anne Bancroft, Carl Reiner, Dom De Luise, Bert Convy, Charles Nelson Reilly, Loni Anderson, Michelle Lee, Norman Fell . . . (get an idea of the types?) . . . along with spouses and mates. Turn this group loose in a room with a blackboard and a piece of chalk, and it's black belt comedy time.

Before play begins, the women gather in one room and the men in another to choose movie and television show titles that the opposing team will be called upon to sketch . . . the more obscure, the more diabolically difficult, the better. Once the titles are decided on, we all get back together to start the game. One by one, each person is given a title to "draw" on the blackboard, for fellow team members to guess, against the clock. Charles Nelson Reilly was timekeeper only once, which was a sketch in itself. Clint Eastwood, who can seem so grim and intense and dignified, was just as ridiculous as the rest of us.

One night, at our house this time, Fred Astaire, who *loves* games, was playing this drawing madness for the first time. (Imagine all these alleged grown-ups, racing through dinner so they can set up their blackboard and play!) Fred was given a title to sketch . . . *Follow the Fleet*, one of his own hit movies.

On this big blackboard, Fred began drawing microscopic little sailors that no one could possibly see. When that didn't work, he drew every kind of ship he could think of, then arrows to try and get them to say, "Follow." This went on for six minutes, and by now his team members were purposely not guessing even if they did know. Finally, in desperation, Fred picked up the entire blackboard and stalked out of the room, as everyone at long last chorused, *"Follow the Fleet!!"*

Not long ago, Burt Reynolds and Bert Convy joined forces to try and put this game on television, and we taped a pilot show. By the time you read this it will be on the air. Some of the drawings, I fear, will lose a little something in the translation to family TV.

Carol Burnett is another game player beyond redemption. Whether there are four people or forty, Carol will have a game afoot.

One night we were invited to her house for an evening of "murder" . . . a game wherein one member of the group is secretly designated as the killer, and it is up to the rest of us to track him down. This is done through a series of *elaborate* clues that have been planted all over the house. Carol must have worked all day setting things up.

Allen's "Password" taping had run a little late, and coming straight from the studio, we arrive just after the game has begun. As we pull up in front of the house, here is Rock Hudson, diligently searching through the bushes by the front door. With a quick "hi" and a wave, he is back to the bushes. We walk in the open front door in time to see Vicki Lawrence running in one direction and Tim Conway in the other. From the top of the stair-way, Carol calls down, "Hi, Allen. Hi, Betty . . . your packets are on the table . . . see you later!" Dutifully, we got our envelopes containing our instructions, and were instantly involved, searching for our own clues . . . for the next hour and a half.

I don't recall whodunit, or who won . . . all I remember is that in following the clues, I kept running into other people doing the same thing, and each one was a famous face! When we all finally got together for refreshments later, it looked as if the party had been done by Central Casting.

For the past fifteen years I have served on the board of GLAZA, the Greater Los Angeles Zoo Association, with Gloria Stewart, a dynamite lady and wife of actor James Stewart. They are both staunch supporters of the zoo with both time and money. One day when Allen had occasion to call their home, Jimmy answered the phone . . . it wasn't too tough to recognize his voice. Allen kidded him, "Don't you know big stars never answer their own phones?" "Well," said Jimmy, "I . . . uh . . . no . . . I guess *they* don't."

Whenever I call Lucille Ball, I have to be careful. More than once, hearing the deep "Hello," I've said, "Gary?" "No, this is Lucille."

With all the various animal activities in which I am involved, I am forever swearing my friends into service. Their marquis value helps immeasurably, and is deeply appreciated. *No one* have I taken more advantage of than

my friend Mary Tyler Moore. Poor Mary must shudder
whenever she hears I'm into a new project, because she
knows it won't be long before she gets my call.

At one point I did a television series called "The Pet
Set" . . . each half hour featured a celebrity with his
pet, and then I would write the rest of the show around
his particular area of interest in animals. Well . . .
guess who my first show was written for! And, as always,
Mary said okay.

First, we interviewed Mary, on camera, with her two
poodles, Maude and Diswilliam . . . and then had a
bevy of poodles of every size, color, age, and flavor ex-
tant. For the big finish, we had our wild animal spot . . .
and I thought it would be fun to do a takeoff on the MTM
pussycat logo.

This was a lovely excuse, (as was the entire show) for
me to romp with special friends of mine . . . Major, a
dear, kind, black-maned lion . . . and Sultan, a Siberian
tiger, whose manners were perfect.

The payoff came with Mary and Betty, sitting on the
floor playing with two six-week-old tiger cubs, and Mary
telling me that the MTM mewing kitten was, in itself, a
takeoff on the original MGM Leo the Lion.

I was thrilled with the way it all tied in, as was everyone
connected with the show. Good friend, Mary, went along
with it, and handled baby tigers' sharp little claws, as well
as Betty's enthusiasm, and kept smiling. It was only after
we signed off that I learned that although Mary loves
animals, cats were anything but her favorites, and the
wild variety were even lower on her totem pole.

Our friendship not only withstood that test, but a couple of years later, lucky Mary got elected to help Betty with yet another adventure.

Because I wanted to show the world what a truly spectacular zoo we have in Los Angeles, I wrote, sold, and hosted a ninety-minute special . . . "Backstage at the Zoo" . . . for the Metromedia stations around the country.

Divided into segments, each segment was hosted by a star/friend . . . Joe Campanella, Amanda Blake, Jimmy Stewart, Greg Morris, and who *else* but Mary Tyler Supportive Buddy Moore!

I wanted to make it fun for her, so she was featured on the baby animal nursery segment. During the interview portion, zoo director Dr. Warren Thomas, Betty, and Mary . . . Mary holding a rambunctious baby gorilla . . . sat in a lovely area outside the zoo nursery, talking about how important these captive-born gorilla babies are to the dwindling worldwide gorilla population. It was a heavy discussion, and midway through, Mary jumped perceptibly. Keeping that uranium MTM smile, she firmly handed baby gorilla to me, yet never missed a beat in the conversation. It seems that the little one found Mary's T-shirt irresistible, and pinched whatever he could find to get her attention.

It is rather amazing that she continues to be such a good friend. Mary is one of those *special* people . . . who are there for you, not just for the good times, but whenever they are really needed.

After tigers and gorillas, I'll have to think of something spectacular for her next time.

And there will be a next time.

On Fans in General

The term "fan" sounds far too impersonal to describe the many many nice people who greet you . . . not as a stranger, but as someone they have invited into their homes. They may not write letters, perhaps, but do take the opportunity to say hello if they happen to see you.

Quite a few ask for autographs . . . and it is interesting to sort out the various ways in which this is done. Attitudes are highly contagious.

The smaller the group . . . the better the manners.

If it is one individual, alone, it's usually "Could I trouble you for an autograph?" or "Would you mind signing this, please?" With pleasure.

If somebody shoves a pencil and paper in your face, shouting, "Sign this!" . . . he or she is asking for a more brusque response. A pushy *group* . . . drawing support and false courage in numbers . . . is usually made up of remarkably normal individuals, who would never act that way on their own. Those who are downright rude, are few and far between.

Then there is the well-meaning soul who eagerly asks for an autograph . . . but doesn't have pencil *or* paper.

Whichever side of the autograph book we happen to be on . . . giving or receiving . . . it's a good idea to remember what a lasting impression can be made in such a brief encounter. It's really too bad that it is the couple of negative examples that stick in your mind rather than all those very nice people you see every day.

Do I have any specifics? Afraid so.

My husband Allen and I were having dinner one night at a very lovely restaurant, in a cozy booth, out of the traffic pattern. We were, as usual, deep in conversation, enjoying each other and the fact that we were out on one of our "married dates."

A woman came up to the table, and in a voice that would cut steel, proclaimed to the world, "It's Allen Ludden! And Betty White!" She went on to say what would normally be some flattering things, but not at those decibels, and not at such length. Foolishly, we assumed we were rescued when the waiter brought our entree. No such luck. He kept trying to maneuver around her, and finally, when he had said, "Excuse me," for the third time, she, without missing a beat in her monologue, sat down in the booth *with* us . . . and there she remained even after the waiter left.

My usually good-natured husband had finally had it, and said, politely but firmly, "Ma'am, your dinner must be getting cold. I know ours is. I suggest you go back to your table now." It didn't seem to shake her even slightly . . . without any show of haste, she got up and left us with, "No, we're done, we're just on coffee. I'll bring my husband over on the way out." I dug my nails into Allen's thigh under the table, just to remind him that it probably wouldn't be nice to hit a lady in a fine restaurant.

I'd like to say she had just had a little too much to drink and was feeling convivial, but I'm afraid she was cold sober and insensitive. We also had the distinct impression that it wasn't Allen and Betty she was gushing over,

but that *anybody* she recognized sitting there would have
been equally lucky. Happy to report, we never did see the
poor guy who had to go home with that woman.

The prize exasperating encounter happened in New
York one chilly night when Allen and I had been married
a short month. Romantic fella that he was, Allen celebrated each month's wedding anniversary with a gift
. . . for the whole first year of our marriage. Of course, I
didn't know that on this first month celebration . . . all
I knew was that we were going to the theater. But when
he came to help me on with my coat, my husband slipped
a short white mink jacket on my shoulders instead. It was
gorgeous, and I was thrilled beyond description.

(AUTHOR'S NOTE: This was in 1963, before it dawned on
either of us how stupid it was to wear fur at the painful
cost of animal lives . . . especially when there are so
many beautiful and warm alternatives.)

We were just stepping into a cab to begin our festive
evening when a young man rushed up, and with a "Hey!
Sign this!" shoved an autograph book and a fountain pen
at me. Now I know why it is called a fountain pen . . . it
literally erupted, with bright blue ink, all down the front
of my brand-new jacket. And I mean *all* down the front!

Undaunted, the young man insisted. "Sign it!" Needless to say, we left him insisting, and rushed back inside
to try and rectify the damage, but it was a mess. Later, the
cleaner tried valiantly . . . they got rid of the blue, but
there remained a sickly yellow stain that proved permanent.

Today, of course, I would read the above and snarl,
"Serves her right for wearing fur!" But at the time I was

unenlightened . . . and, in any event, his blue ink
wouldn't have looked good on whatever I was wearing.

Enough of the bad news, let's get back to something
more pleasant.

Fan clubs have been in existence for a long long time,
but over the years they have grown larger, both in size
and number, as well as more sophisticated. They usually
begin with a few people who like the same celebrity, and
this forms the nucleus of a mutual admiration society.
These groups have proliferated to the point that there is
now an International Society of Fan Clubs . . . members of different individual clubs meet and mingle at the
annual convention.

There has been a Betty White fan club for over thirty
years, which has remained loyal and supportive through
all the different stages of my career. Called "Bets' Pets,"
it was originally started by a girl viewer, Barbara Guthrie,
who went on to become my first secretary. The club has
been in the capable hands of one Kay Daly, its president,
ever since. Kay is a busy and dedicated fourth grade
teacher, yet still finds the time to run the club, send out a
monthly newsletter, and a yearly journal. "Bets' Pets" is
not only self-sustaining, but each Christmas, and again
on my birthday, a charity fund is raised and sent to various animal organizations in my honor. These people are
all give and no take . . . asking nothing of me, either
financially or in terms of time. Fan clubs are misunder-
stood and underestimated by many as simply an ego trip
for the celebrity involved. I can only judge from the
"Pets," but I see them as individuals with common interests who reach out across the country, becoming pen

pals with each other, forming lasting friendships, and enjoying their hobby. I have found my fan club to be a group of constant and loyal friends through good times and bad. They are much appreciated.

Since we haven't been able to come up with anything better than the term "fan," I guess we're stuck with it. "Devotees" sounds pretentious . . . "followers" has a cultish ring to it . . . "supporters" won't do at all. Sports fans would then become "athletic supporters."

No . . . "fans" it shall be . . . and thank God for them.

On Fan Mail

There is also something vaguely unsavory to me about the term "fan letter." It always sounds like a putdown of the sender, the recipient . . . or both. However, since I can't seem to come up with anything better . . . "letters from unknown strangers"?, "strange letters"?, "letters I've never met"? . . . let's, under protest, go with "fan mail."

A percentage of the mail that comes in consists of simple requests for autographed pictures. A very few of these get quite specific, even a tad demanding. "Send me an 8 × 10, personally signed, not Xeroxed!" "Please" may or may not be added as an afterthought. (For the record, I sign 'em all. No Xeroxes.)

Another larger portion of the mail asks for personalized items to sell at charity auctions. This is a phenomenon that has mushroomed in just the last few years, until now these requests number in the dozens each week, and growing. With some exceptions . . . (I couldn't resist the little girl who asked for an item to sell at their celebrity "option") . . . it is regrettably impossible to respond to them all. The goose is running low on golden eggs.

Many of my letters, naturally, have to do with animals in some way . . . requesting information, inviting me to various fund-raisers, reporting abuses, or simply sharing pictures of their pets with me. You can guess the ones I like best.

Now and then there will be the direct pitch for money. Not a little money . . . this group always seems to think in terms of five figures. Usually there is some fail-safe product they are trying to launch. But once in a while there is the hardy soul who just asks for the money . . . period. I often wonder if any of these ever receive an answer. Not from me.

Whatever term we use for it, the mail comes in from a wide assortment of viewers of all ages, colors, occupations, economic levels, incarcerations, political or sexual persuasions. It furnishes those of us on television a chance to look back through the TV screen and see who's out there . . . sometimes even to get acquainted.

I still receive letters from people who have been writing to me for thirty years. Most of them I have never met, and my responses are pitifully meager and infrequent, but they continue to write without complaint. I've gone through their marriages and divorces, watched their children grow . . . in a couple of cases we're on our third generation.

One unforgettable lady wrote to me every single week for almost fifteen years. Her name was Evelyn Martin, and her letter would come in *without fail* every Monday morning . . . one sheet, written on both sides. When she came to the bottom of the page, even if she was in the middle of a sentence, the letter would stop with "Love, Evelyn." She would tell me about her friends, and her club meetings, but almost never about herself. She lived in Heltonville, Indiana, which, she once explained to me, was halfway between Bridgeport and Seymour! The only way I learned that she didn't have running water in her house was when everyone's pipes froze one year and they all had to come to the pump at her back door.

For years I didn't have a clue as to Evelyn's age or appearance, then she finally sent me a picture of herself . . . a tiny, blurry snapshot . . . a friend had taken on her fifty-fourth birthday.

For Evelyn, the whole year revolved around Christmas. She would make it last until spring, then immediately begin pointing for the next "Yuletide," as she always called it.

It continually amazed me that her letters never missed being on time . . . every Monday morning . . . even when I moved to New York for six years after Allen and I were married. Which event, incidentally, almost caused a break in Evelyn's loyal friendship. When she heard that I had married Allen Ludden, the letters didn't stop, but were filled with her shock and deep disappointment that I had broken up a man's home and family. And shame on him, too! Love, Evelyn! I lost no time assuring her that Allen was a widower, and had been since I'd known him. She not only forgave me, but took Allen into the fold as well. In true Allen fashion, because he enjoyed her letters so, he saw to it that she received a Della Robbia wreath every Christmas. She kept them from year to year.

One Monday, instead of Evelyn's familiar writing, I received a note from her neighbor . . . Evelyn had died in her sleep.

A letter came in just recently from another longtime correspondent . . . a lady in Wisconsin who has been writing to me for over twenty years. Again, my responses are almost nonexistent, but her letters have always been long and newsy . . . full of stories about her husband, their boat, and their pets. Five years ago, her husband was diagnosed as having Alzheimer's disease, and he finally had to be put in a nursing home. This story is better told by the lady herself, so let me quote her letter:

"Having researched and written *Pet Love*, thought you might be interested in some more findings on the subject.

"George's brain has been destroyed . . . he is now like a nine-month-old infant. He's forgotten how to talk, walk, read, write, or care for himself. He doesn't know me, or recognize the nurses who give him tender loving care . . .

"In December I found the collar of George's tan Chihuahua, Amigo, with the ID tag AMIGO—I BELONG TO

GEORGE LOW and the leash with Amigo's last 1978 license. I put them on a toy stuffed Scotty dog and took them to the nursing home.

"At first there was no response from George to us or the toy. He just had a dead man's stare. Several days later, the nurse and aides were so excited, asking me to see George, who was petting and babbling to the toy . . . He smiled and cooed with glee, trying to tell us about his dog, but we couldn't understand a word.

"For a long time he had been fanning the floor with his hand, but no longer does that. He must have been petting his dogs, but now with a dog to hold, he no longer needs to pet unseen dogs on the floor. They put the leash around his waist, so if he drops the dog he can bring it back to himself. They say they put Amigo to bed with him, so if he wakes up in the night he has his dog . . . He seems more alert to his surroundings for the past two months. It is pet therapy even with a toy pet!"

With the advent of "The Golden Girls," the mail has increased in volume and the horizons have expanded, as we are seen in so many different countries . . . but the breakdown remains fairly consistent. Already there are some regulars beginning to surface . . . a young man in England who keeps me posted on our ratings over there . . . a chap from Australia who sends animal pictures . . . as well as the one-timers.

My secretary and right arm, Gail Clark, handles opening and sorting and simple requests, but she sees that I read the personals. And our ironclad rule is that I see every single negative letter. There are some, of course, but these are a surprisingly small minority. With today's tendency toward negativism, I am always amazed that so many people take the time to sit down and say what they *liked* . . . and, believe me, it is appreciated. Unfortunately, once again it is the bad ones that stick in your mind. It is not to my credit that the one I remember most mentioned each and every thing about me they couldn't stand, and documented all my individual performances over the years that they had hated . . . *watched* but hated. Jellyfish that I am, it cut right to the bone. (All *right!* Jellyfish don't have bones, but you know what I mean!) Whenever I start getting carried away with myself, I think about that letter.

And then there are the obscene letters. Or, in my case, letter. I have heard celebrity friends talk about them, and know they can be a real problem. It says something about me . . . (I'm not sure *what!*) . . . that, though I have received several threats, and a few marriage proposals, I have received only one bona fide obscene letter . . . and it was mimeo'd!

Jellyfish that I am . . . !

On Professional Jealousy

Professional jealousy. How is that for a classic cliché? Unfortunately, that doesn't make it any less valid. While it is to be found in any field of endeavor, show biz takes the biggest rap . . . sometimes warranted, sometimes not.

There are few lines of work wherein a person is as vulnerable, or as desperately in need of approval, as in the acting game. The touchy psyche that is the basis of whatever talent may exist is about as stable as a sea anemone . . . wide open in full bloom one moment, then, without visible provocation, collapsing within itself the next.

We may attempt to hide the situation by wearing a number of disguises . . . overconfidence, sickening humility, indifference . . . but those are only the costumes. Gut-level insecurity is the reality . . . and for good reason. Despite how diligently he may work to hone his craft, there is really no solid ground on which an actor can stand . . . because he cannot lock in his *best* performance, then know it will be that way every time. He keeps "improving" it . . . once in a while it even gets better . . . often, only bigger.

How, then, do these fragile egos . . . these tissue-paper-skinned individuals . . . ever manage to work together? Sometimes they don't very well.

It always saddens me to hear that some highly successful show is a hotbed of dissension in real life . . . or that the stars of this or that series are, in fact, carrying on a running feud. How do you *work* under those conditions . . . let alone turn out a decent product?

Some of the stories, to be sure, are apocryphal. Because gossip is mother's milk to a great many people, a whole industry of garbage newspapers flourishes at every market checkout stand in the country. Writing about how well people get along doesn't sell very well, so if it's a slow feud day, they make some up!

Sad to say, there are times when rumors are based on fact. Knowing how much time and togetherness is involved in making a television series, it is mind-boggling to think of doing it if you disliked each other! Bad enough in a dramatic situation . . . imagine doing *comedy* under those conditions?!

I don't even want to contemplate what the set of "The Golden Girls" would be like if we didn't all support and respect one another. The fact that we also happen to be nuts about each other was an added starter which could not have been foreseen when the show was first put together.

Beatrice Arthur and Rue McClanahan had worked together for six years on "Maude" . . . Rue and I had been on "Mama's Family" together for a couple of seasons . . . Estelle Getty came from a hot run on Broadway in *Torch Song Trilogy*. There could not *be* four more disparate females! If you think Dorothy, Blanche, Sophia, and Rose differ from each other on the *show* . . . that's nothing compared to what we are in person. Yet we hit it off from the word go.

It isn't hard to figure out the reason . . . or *reasons* for that. The four of us came together, each with an established career in place . . . past the stage (and age) of desperately trying to carve our own niche in the business. We were all interested in the show itself, not just

our own characters . . . thanks to the wise producers
and writers. They pulled off a real hat trick, by giving
each of those characters enough to do in every script to
keep us very busy and out of trouble.

From the very beginning, we were each thrilled by the
professionalism of the other three. No one had to be carried. Whatever one of us served up was returned in kind
. . . or better.

Of equal importance, if a set is to be a happy one, we
were also blessed by the work manners of our group. No
one had to be waited for . . . each was *where* she was
supposed to be *when* she was supposed to be there. This
set the tone and allowed us to relax and get silly, knowing that when the whistle blew, we'd all be in the chute.

You cannot imagine what a luxury that is for an actor.
And I have been so very lucky . . . this was not my first
experience with such an ideal work situation. "The Mary
Tyler Moore Show" had the same degree of professionalism . . . and deep friendship.

The tone of *that* show was set by the lady herself.
Mary's talent, integrity . . . not to mention her punctu-
ality . . . gave everyone else something to shoot for.
She was, in every positive sense of the word, the star of
the show. The show ran for seven years . . . I came
aboard for the last four, but only on a part-time basis.
The most scripts in one twenty-two week season in which
rotten Sue Ann Nivens appeared was twelve . . . but
she was there for that final show. That's when the love
really spilled over, and we were awash all week . . .
laughing a lot, and crying a *lot.*

The writers couldn't bring themselves to actually put

the final scene down on paper until two days before the
show. Jay Sandrich, our wonderful director, couldn't
handle rehearsing it (any more than we could) until the
very day of the filming. We all cried through rehearsal,
we all cried at performance . . . even during a pickup
shot afterward.

Six weeks later, Mary invited us to Chasen's for what
she called a "TV dinner" . . . so we could all finally see
the show before it aired, and be able to see what we had
done.

There were television monitors at the tables . . .
only those *directly* involved in the show were there that
night . . . and we laughed up a storm. We hadn't realized it at the time, but it was a very funny episode. Then
came the final scene, and we all got rather quiet, but we
were still okay . . . until Lou Grant said, "I treasure you
people!" The sob was in unison!

As a result, to this day, many many reruns later, I have
yet to see that scene except underwater.

We filmed the series on the MTM lot that began as the
Mack Sennett Studio. We shot all the episodes on one of
the original sound stages . . . which had started out as
comedienne Mabel Normand's home base back in the
twenties. On a bronze plaque to the left of the big stage
door, in honor of Miss Normand, it says:

We dedicate this stage to the memory of a lovable
artist. May we never forget her. A great soul who
pioneered and gave purpose to the early motion
picture. Through this new art she brought laughter
and beauty otherwise denied millions burdened
with despair and drabness.

After Mary's closing episode was filmed, another bronze plaque was placed to the right of that same big stage door, reading:

On this stage a company of loving and talented friends produced a TV classic. "The Mary Tyler Moore Show," 1970–1977.

Any show that manages to keep everyone happy is rare enough when it is a one-star situation . . . but multiply that by four, make them all females, and it could be a nightmare. Especially for the poor director, who is on the front line with these potential dragons. Once again, "The Golden Girls" producers, Paul Witt, Tony Thomas, and Susan Harris, have pulled off a miracle. We have been given a director, Terry Hughes, at whose feet we openly worship . . . and his firm hand on the reins is so unobtrusive, we are all convinced we are getting our own way.

Interviewers repeatedly want to know what I would really dream of doing in this business, if I could choose anything I wanted. I can't ever seem to get the point across that I am *doing* it . . . right *now!*

Over the years, there have been some tremendously successful television shows where, after the first hue and cry, tedium sets in. One or another cast member gets claustrophobic and defects, to go in search of bigger and better things. Some have discovered, too late, that the water outside is deep and cold. There are so many diverse, private, and often valid reasons that have a bearing on that defection that it is impossible to generalize and say it was a dumb thing to do. But if the reason was jealousy . . . it *was*.

There doesn't seem to be any special age at which professional jealousy is finally outgrown. Some actors, old enough to know better, can't say anything good about anyone else in their category. On the other hand, youth and inexperience are often components in the problem. That's understandable . . . lack of seasoning, and sometimes bad advice, can warp a young performer's perspective, until he begins to believe that someone else, less talented, got the good breaks that he deserved . . . or worse . . . that he deserved the breaks he got. There is no cure for this particular work hazard . . . some succumb to it . . . some overcome it . . . and some never had it in the first place.

When the sitcom "Happy Days" began, I don't believe anyone could have expected the Fonz to take off quite as much as he did . . . so it might have been understandable if Ron Howard had resented it ever so slightly. The Fonz himself, Henry Winkler, could also have become a little insufferable. Instead, being the class acts they both are, they worked together as mutually talented friends. It is not surprising that both continue to carve increasingly important places for themselves in the producing and directing field, as well as acting.

Michael J. Fox is another whose career took off like a rocket. However, far from deserting television after his successes on the big screen . . . he not only remains

with "Family Ties," but says he will be there as long as
the show exists.

So much for youth's so-called warped perspective!

At this writing, Bea, and Rue, and Estelle and I, together with Terry Hughes, have been working together
for two full seasons . . . fifty-one shows in all so far. If
we haven't gotten in trouble with each other by now, I
think it highly unlikely we ever will. I can only hope we'll
be hanging in there together for many more seasons to
come . . . the network, the public, and God willing.

On Competition

Professional jealousy may be nothing more than healthy
competition that is stagestruck.

Wasn't it during the sixties that "competition" became
such a dirty word? And "pride" . . . there was another
one. "Too much competition" was the battle cry . . .
and became the scapegoat for practically every sin
known to man.

It's the "too much" that seems to be the villain from
where I sit. We are a too much society on virtually (hardly
the right word) every front. For one thing, we spend too
much time talking about it.

But why must competition take the rap? And what's so
bad about pride in a job well done?

Fortunately, the proverbial pendulum seems to be swinging back to the point where the competitive spirit is almost returning to favor . . . just as well, because where would we begin to eliminate it from our lives?

New parents compete to see who can elicit baby's first smile.

Drivers compete from the moment they get behind the wheel.

And . . . as any television viewer worth his salt can tell you . . . housewives are in a constant swivet as to who has the whitest wash!

Facetious examples are a cheap shot . . . I do not mean to make light of a serious subject. Stress is a killer . . . and much of that stress comes from simply trying to make it through the day in our competitive world.

Ideally, competition on the job, or in school, should serve as an incentive to make us try a little harder, or reach a little farther. Unfortunately, nothing ever works quite the way it's supposed to. If the pressures exerted are inordinate . . . or what's even worse . . . if everyone isn't playing by the rules, the results can be, and often are, tragic.

But if we can't lick competition . . . join it! Turn it around and make it work *for* us.

Dieters find solace in challenging a buddy to see who can lose the most poundage in a given time.

Some smokers find it easier to go longer without a cigarette if they are trying to beat someone else.

Ret Turner, one of TV's Emmy-winning costume designers, made a hefty bet with a friend that he could go a whole year without chocolate. As of now, he is in the seventh month of the bet . . . alternately stalwart, then drooling . . . however, he admits he never could have done it on his own. Ret realizes, better than anyone, that he is really competing with *himself*. But to call it old-fashioned willpower would take all the fun out of it . . . he would slip off the chocolate wagon in no time.

In show business, competition is the name of the game . . . purely by the nature of the industry itself. The fact that we showfolk must thrive on it is indicated by the staggering number of award shows designed to celebrate the best of our best. Here, the competition is rife . . . but, hopefully, healthy. There is only one winner in each category . . . but if you've made it that far . . . there are *no* losers. I can't buy the fact that show business is *more* competitive than most other callings . . . we just have a higher profile.

Don't you think that most winners wind up really only competing with *themselves* over the long haul?

Competing against yourself, day by day, stretches your capabilities and allows you to grow . . . just don't make the standards too high. Remember, the object is to wind up feeling good about yourself . . . so the goal must be attainable . . . the rest is up to you. Of course, there's no law against raising the sights from time to time . . . as long as they remain within reach.

Oh . . . and it's very important to be a good winner. Pounding one's opponent into the ground is frowned on at best . . . but it's an especially bad idea when *you* are your opponent.

Granted, I get a little carried away in the competition

department. Sometimes, when I'm taking a shower, I try and see how many times I can flip the soap in one hand without dropping it . . . then try and beat the number with the other hand. Tomorrow, I try and better the score. It does sound a little weird on the face of it, I have to admit . . . but it's *great* for the upper arms. No one knows better than I that there isn't much of a call for soap-flipping . . . it is simply a ridiculous example of trying to do something better for its own sake, without having someone standing over you . . . which would be particularly unseemly in my shower.

Taken to its logical . . . and certainly less frivolous extension, the philosophy of *healthy* competition makes for personal pride in accomplishment. Carried over into the workplace, it means you do what you do . . . what*ever* that may be . . . to the best of your ability, just because it makes *you* feel good.

That is far too simple an antidote to be an effective cure for job disinterest and shoddy workmanship. A great deal of research, time, and money is being spent these days, trying to find a way to instill pride in performance in the current work force. Strange that it's such a hard sell to put across the idea that whatever you do . . . at work or at play . . . is not only more interesting if you do it the best you possibly can . . . but the time slips by so much faster.

Being compulsive about anything is a fairly bum idea, and I guess the work ethic is no exception. Moderation is the answer, as we learned in Shangri-La, but it's not that easy . . . that damned pendulum never stops in the

middle. We are not only immoderate about what's bad
for us . . . we even have a tough time taking the middle
road with things that are supposed to be *good*.

How do you rein in a workaholic? Or how do you fire
up a drone?

There are those to whom work is a four-letter word.
These types spend a great deal of effort and creative
energy putting in as little time on it as possible. Nonwork
to them is nirvana . . . which would be swell, if they
didn't also refer to their *off*-time as *bor-ring!* Evidently,
even *not* working is too much effort.

These people are not the same breed of cat as the folk
who purposefully abstain from work altogether . . .
your dedicated beachcomber . . . your career surfer
. . . your card-carrying knight of the road. This group
elevates not being gainfully employed to an art form.
They don't complain about it . . . they celebrate it.

By way of contrast . . . at the other end of the spec-
trum are those suffering from chronic workaholism.
Someday I'm sure it will be included in the list of bona
fide social diseases. It is truly incurable.

The White Rabbit would be perfect for the part. The
workaholic works *all* the time. At *something*. Always hurry-
ing to finish the job at hand in order to rush to the next,
during which time a new project is taking place in his
. . . or her . . . head. I plead guilty to this persuasion,
but I came by it naturally.

My father was never satisfied with doing just two
things at once if he could possibly squeeze in a third.
Mom used to call him "Hurry Horace, the Humming-

bird." I can still hear her . . . "Honey, do you think you can light long enough to eat dinner?"

Dad's time *off* was the same. Like Allen, he too was a gardener, and on weekends this meant he was out there at dawn, and working like a field hand, until, at the other end of the day, it got too dark to see. He did come in midmorning for our threesome brunch, where we would gab about everything under the sun. But it wasn't long before he would begin to chafe at the bit to get back outside.

Dad's job was his pride and joy. In the forty-five years he spent with the Crouse-Hinds Company . . . selling floodlights, traffic signals, explosion-proof fittings for the Navy . . . he went from office boy to commercial vice president. There was a mandatory retirement age of sixty-five, and he used to make a lot of noise about how he didn't mind that at all. He had big plans for his retirement . . . travel, various projects . . . but somehow they all had a rather hollow ring. Dad's problem was solved when he died six months before his sixty-fifth birthday. I've often wondered if he might just have been scared to death.

It's a pattern with which I can readily identify . . . I'm just luckier than he was, in that there is no retirement age stipulation in my line of work. I hope to hang around playing *something* as long as I am able to stand up. As far as my animal work is concerned, the animals don't care how old I get. So I am much better off than my dad.

But my social life does take something of a beating at times. I keep saying, "Things will let up soon as I finish this . . . or that . . . or something else." My closest friend shakes his head in complete disgust . . . "Until you start working on the next thing!"

The more angrily I deny it, the more I know in my heart he's right.

I'll work on it.

On Laughter

At last it has been officially established that laughter is beneficial to one's health and well-being. Well, that takes a big load off my mind . . . most of the things I like to do are so bad for me.

And I do love to laugh. Thank Heaven I'm in the funny business. Although it often surprises me how serious many comedians are about comedy. Not all, I'm happy to say . . . but more than I ever suspected.

The late comedian and television host Hal March used to come on my first series, "Life with Elizabeth," as a guest star . . . when we could afford one. He and Del Moore, who played my husband Alvin on the show, and I used to laugh so much together that the filming would run overtime. But Hal was irrepressible and Del was no help. I was dignified and perfect.

Hal was the first to point out the fact that everybody didn't have as much fun working as we did. He used to say, "Put five comics in a room together telling jokes . . . there are no laughs . . . only frowns. Somebody will tell a joke, and one frowner will comment, 'That's funny.' Another joke, and somebody else will frown, 'Now, that's *very* funny. That's hysterical.' They don't have time to laugh, they are busy filing the jokes away in their heads."

I like the laughers better.

Breakups onstage, or in the studio, are devastating . . . to the person involved . . . as well as everyone else onstage at the time. The more prone a person is to this sort of thing, the tighter rein he must hold on himself. Or herself!!!

The problem is, you never know when something is going to happen that will set you off. Ninety-nine percent of the time it isn't even anything particularly funny . . . but when it hits, you are helpless. The harder you try to shape up, the funnier everything gets.

Now, you would expect an idiot like me to have this weakness . . . and, God knows, I do. But the *least* likely person in the world, with all her wonderful professionalism, I have seen turn into a mess before my very eyes . . . my tall friend Beatrice Arthur.

It doesn't happen often . . . maybe three or four times in the past two seasons. There are no warning signals, and no sound . . . but you know you are in trouble when you throw Bea a cue and get no answer. You turn and find that she is *beet* red, with tears streaming

down her face, and she is going through these parox-
ysms, but making no noise whatever . . . just helpless
little gestures with her hands.

Of course, it is contagious and spreads like wildfire
through the cast. We finally pull ourselves together to go
on with the scene . . . but the damage has been done.
From then on . . . (we rehearse for a week before taping) . . . every single time we get to that spot in the
script, Bea is *gone*. It happens all over again, each time,
and she is helpless . . . this controlled, dignified, con-
summate actress! By the time we get to the actual taping,
she manages to get through . . . but there is absolutely
no eye contact between any of us until we are past the
danger zone.

What starts it? Who *knows* what strikes a funny bone
with anybody? One time it was a line in the script that hit
Bea funny. The plot was: Sophia was accepting an award.
We were all at this banquet where Don Johnson was to
appear. He couldn't make it . . . but they introduced
his clothes!! That may not do it for you, but Bea col-
lapsed every time.

What makes it so marvelous in her case is that normally Bea is not a laugher. She may enjoy a joke with a
smile, maybe a small chuckle . . . she is more likely to
react to a funny remark with a deadpan stare. It's just
such *fun* to see her fall apart! Rue said that once when
they were taping "Maude" they finally shut down for the
afternoon and sent everybody home . . . they simply
couldn't straighten up.

It may tickle you when it happens to somebody else,
but, having been there, it can be a killer. The more you

try to stop, or the harder you bite your cheek, or the sadder the mental images you try and conjure up . . . the more hysterical everything becomes.

By now, I'm sure you are thinking that they should throw a net over all of us, and you're probably right. Just keep in mind, we are not in the most stable line of work.

Connie Chung, the excellent television newsperson, was on locally here in California before going network. Connie has a delicious sense of humor, but is, to be sure, all business when reporting the news. There were, however, some rare occasions on the early evening news in Los Angeles that were memorable. A slight stumble in words, on her part or someone else's . . . meaning to say one thing, but something else came out . . . could set her off.

Watching her lose the battle with herself was worth the price of admission. At first, she would try and ride it out by ignoring it, a deep serious frown suddenly appearing between her eyes . . . but then her voice would tighten, and she would lose it. Momentarily, only . . . as she had to keep fighting valiantly from one grim news story to the next.

I would suffer with her, knowing what she was going through. It is one thing to have breakups on a comedy show, but there are a few places where it is just not possible . . . and a news broadcast is one of them. Knowing this doesn't do one thing toward saving you when it counts.

Sometimes a crack-up is caused, with deliberate intent, by one or another diabolical member of the company. In a long-running play, it has been done to relieve the tedium . . . but it is not considered the height of serious theater. In a television studio, the temptations, and the opportunities, are multiplied.

Harvey Korman and Tim Conway are a classic example of two bad boys who should never be allowed to play together. People often thought their breakups on "The Carol Burnett Show" were planned. Not so . . . they were just highly susceptible to each other's humor, and sometimes it took nothing more than walking onstage together to get them going. However, Tim did have a sneaky habit of holding back some little goodie . . . a line, or a reaction, or a special piece of wardrobe . . . that no one had seen in rehearsal. Come airtime, hearing it for the first time, everybody was apt to go up . . . but Harvey was a sure wipeout.

My sympathy for Harve (whom I adore) would be a lot deeper had I not done a play with him, years ago, in Milwaukee summer stock . . . *Who Was That Lady I Saw You With?*

This time, Harvey was the culprit jokester. He spotted me immediately as having a low laugh threshold . . . and he would stoop to anything. At the opening of the second act, each night, I was onstage, alone, pasting pictures in a scrapbook. Somehow Harvey would manage to get to that scrapbook ahead of time, and I never knew *what* to expect when I opened it . . . once it was a row of naked little old ladies in army boots! . . . then he would make his entrance with big innocent eyes waiting for my reaction. This childish six-foot-four person would even glue my coffee cup to the saucer. Now, this was theater-in-the-round, where the audience was not only on all sides of you, but so close, they were practically in your lap . . . there was no place to hide. My only source of comfort was that once, maybe twice, I managed to play it very straight . . . so much so that Harvey cracked himself up! But then, naturally, *that* would do *me* in! This, dear drama students, is *not* the way to run a railroad.

Quite seriously, "fun in the studio" can be a real bore to the audience if they don't know what's going on . . . making them feel left out, and that is nothing short of rude. Through the years, I have tried to make it a policy to deal the audience in and explain what the joke is, either during or after the show. For all the times that circumstances have made this impossible . . . as well as for any future digressions that are bound to occur . . . please accept this as a blanket apology.

I'm not really a bad person. I just got in with the wrong crowd.

III

OUT OF MY MIND

On Imagination

There is one addition I would like to nominate for the Endangered Species list. Imagination.

It has been explained to me at great length, more than once, that in today's world of sophisticated toys and omnipresent television, we have paved over the ground where imagination grew. There is no room for it anymore. Tsk tsk. Too bad. So sad.

Not so fast.

It is difficult for me to agree that today's kids have less imagination . . . I just think sometimes its growth is stunted too early. I'm not talking about programming a computer, or drawing a picture electronically . . . but the ability to visualize something in the mind without having to press a button . . . or to make up a complicated daydream out of whole cloth, without the chemical stimulation of hallucinogens.

Daydreams still allow for the distinction between imagination and reality.

Hallucinations don't.

Remember that period, not too long ago, when the alleged experts were saying how wrong it was to tell children stories . . . or to let them pretend to believe in Santa Claus or the Tooth Fairy for a little while? Unrealistic! they cried . . . that would do the child no end of harm in later life.

Some parents took that to mean it was okay to stick the child in front of TV as an electronic baby-sitter. Others, while not abusing the television alternative, still went all out on the theory of tell-it-like-it-is . . . discouraging daydreams and flights of fancy with a vengeance. Romanticizing was a no-no. Happily, this extreme was current and choice only briefly . . . in the mellowing, poor old Santa and friends are no longer on the hit list.

As the number of child-abuse cases continues to increase, some little ones have OD'd on reality before they can talk . . . and thank God for the people who devote their lives to try and help. That is a devastating and deeply serious subject, and not one we are addressing here.

For those youngsters in an average normal home environment, blend of fact and fiction is still possible. We don't have to throw away the television or CD, providing we monitor those little minds, and continue to make the distinction between show biz and the news. It isn't easy for a healthy (repeat, healthy) imagination to develop these days . . . and it's never too early to nurture it.

Toddlers still go through that inevitable stage when they have more fun with the box a toy came in than with the toy itself. That's the time to get on their wavelength, and try and see what they see. Not to intrude on the game . . . but being a grown-up doesn't automatically rule you out. It does, however, give you the privilege of blowing the whistle at any time . . . don't blow it *too* soon.

Where I find a dearth of imagination today is among those who have attained their full height, but just can't seem to "picture" things. They have lost the ability . . . if they ever had it . . . to see things more than one way. They choose the obvious and never look beyond to see if there is another meaning for a little fun. Forget *doubl'!* . . . you're lucky if you can make it with singl' entendre. I've long suspected that puns are often frowned on simply because people are too lazy to figure them out.

I grew up on the Oz books. A mastoid infection laid me very low when I was little, and my mom and dad would take turns reading them to me. As they finished one, Dad would somehow scrounge enough money . . . around $1.50 . . . to bring home the next one. All three of us were enchanted by them, and certain Oz lines were family jokes all our lives. We were not alone. There is a large International Oz Society . . . of grown-ups.

There are thirty-six Oz books in all. Dipping into them, after all those years, I realize that L. Frank Baum, and later his daughter, Ruth Plumly Thompson, had a way with words that made it fun to see all the different ways they could be used.

At one point . . . somewhere around ten . . . I got so carried away I wrote an Oz story myself, in the form of a screenplay. As I recall, it was something about Mae West landing in Oz, and her subsequent adventures. All I really remember is the title (only one this time) . . . *Trouble in Paradoz.* Maybe that's all there was. A bad memory *can* be a blessing.

Maybe that all had something to do with why I still love

to play word games, both on and off television. More
mental exercise.

Fortunately for me, I lucked into a mother and father
who were tops in the imagination department. For three
of my preteen years we had an imaginary horse . . . Bill
Promise. Invisible though he was, he went with us on our
summer driving vacations. Dad would carefully tie him to
the bumper when we'd start out in the morning, then
untie him and put him to pasture when we pulled in at
night. I had to take care of the feeding.

Remember the beautiful blind horse in the "Ahead
with Horses" program . . . Promise Yourself? Could
he be related to my Bill Promise? In a way . . . maybe
he could.

Another running gag my mother and I had for years
was "Whatif . . . ?" One would start and the other
would have to finish. We'd scare the daylights out of each
other, but we laughed a lot, too.

We'd also play "What did Cleopatra . . . or whoever
. . . do on her day off?" (*Besides* that! Remember, I was
just a little kid!)

If by now you are thinking of throwing a net over me
. . . consider Hugh Downs. He does whole three-act
plays in *his* imagination. He described one of these flights
of fancy to me once.

It seems he was walking through Central Park one
spring day, and as he approached a bench he could see,
from a distance, that seated there was a really lovely girl.
Hugh, a devoted and happy husband to his Ruth, was not

prone to accosting pretty young things in the park . . .
or anywhere else. Keep in mind . . . it was spring . . .
this was fantasy . . . and it all took less time than it does
to tell about it.

As he drew near the bench, he thought to himself,
"Suppose I were to speak to this girl. And what if she had
been watching me, and answers. I linger, caught up in
conversation, and learn that she also is married . . .
and has two children. We are involuntarily drawn to each
other, and fall deeply in love. We realize we must tell our
families if we are to make a life together . . . and we
know how deeply we will hurt all those other innocent
people . . . and what a far-reaching and adverse effect
it will have on all their lives. This in turn will make us
wretched . . . eventually driving us apart." Hugh
sighed, then softly, "So the greatest kindness I could do
this beautiful young woman was to walk on by without a
glance in her direction."

This is the same man we see on "20/20."

This is the same man who once sailed across the Pacific
. . . alone.

If this is all a bit too *Peter Pan* for your taste, I apolo-
gize. I really did grow up . . . honestly I did. So did my
mother and father . . . as did Hugh Downs.

But just imagine the fun we had!

On Habits and Superstition

Wouldn't it be great if we were able to form *good* habits as easily as bad?

Suppose everyone had only good habits. Think of the ramifications.

Drivers would make it a habit to stop when the light turns yellow. Repairmen would make it a habit to fix something on the first trip. Terrorists would form the habit of not planting bombs in Belfast or Beirut.

At first blush it sounds like the ultimate solution to so many things. But, no doubt, there would also be side effects.

For instance, if we only had good habits, what on earth would happen to cocktail party conversation? Can you imagine hearing "I'm determined to quit not smoking" or "I eat such a nutritionally balanced diet, my weight remains perfect!"

Of course, if we only had good habits there might not be a cocktail party in the first place. I may be on to something.

Why are good habits so much more difficult to come by than bad ones? You would think by simply concentrating on doing something right each time . . . whatever it might be . . . it would soon become automatic, and you wouldn't have to give it another conscious thought. Like forming the habit of *always* putting something back where it belongs. One could write a book in the time saved not having to hunt for car keys alone.

And good posture. That could become a habit if you put your mind to it. Shoulders down, chest out, tummy in. I've been concentrating on that for more years than you can count, and . . . trust me . . . it does not become second nature. The older I get the more I tend to confuse the prepositions . . . shoulders up, chest down, tummy out. Perhaps a dowager's hump is inevitable. (In a sense, it could even be something to look forward to.)

Do you make it a habit always to include the name when you jot down a phone number? I keep finding stray numbers on bits of paper under the telephone, or in old purses, and I haven't the foggiest as to whom they belong. One *could* call to check them out if one wanted to feel like an idiot. "Hello. Whom am I calling?" This one really needs work, because I get furious with myself. It doesn't take a mental giant . . . or an extra second . . . to scribble a name along with the number.

Then there are the people to be envied who make it a habit to write notes or answer letters immediately. Their desks must be as clear as their consciences. They realize it is so much easier to scratch off a quick line *now*, than add to the "Must Answer" stack, for when there is more time. When I finally do get around to this group, I spend half a page apologizing for the late response . . . and by then, I'm out of time again.

Bob Barker, busy as he is, gets a gold star in this

department. On a couple of occasions I've sent him a
note or congratulatory telegram . . . and there is an
answer in the return mail . . . handwritten, warm, and
to the point. There are no apologies for tardiness, no
lengthy explanations to wade through . . . he says what
he means to say, then gets off.

I'll keep working on it, but it may mean deep-sixing the
present backlog and starting from scratch. Even I know
that when the paper begins to yellow, it's a symptom that
I've waited too long.

No two ways about it . . . habits are difficult to form
on purpose. You have to just slip into them . . . like old
bedroom slippers.

If habit and superstition are not married, they have
certainly been going together for a very long time.
Sometimes it's hard to determine where the line of de-
marcation falls.

What set me thinking about this heavy subject, was
watching our "Golden Girls" company in action . . .
not just the Girls themselves, but the producers, the
director, the writers, and the production staff, as well.

At our studio, there is a small area, off the control
room, called the Producer's Booth. Comfortably furnished, with overstuffed couches and chairs, it is where
the producers watch the show during the actual taping.
They prefer to watch it on the monitor, so they see it
from the same perspective as the home audience.

Each week, we have a dress rehearsal on Thursday
evening, directly following the day of camera blocking
. . . and, by now, the show should be almost in final
shape for the taping on Friday. When we finish the dress,

we meet with the producers and director . . . in the
Producer's Booth . . . to go over the script, page by
page, and get our final notes.

We have done this for fifty-one shows, now. The first
week we did it, we all walked into the Booth and sat
down, at random, in whatever places were available. The
second week, we peeled off into the same places, without
giving it a thought. By the third week, a visiting guest star
sat down in the spot usually occupied by one of our
producers. Without realizing what we were doing, we all
started milling around, trying unsuccessfully to get settled. It was like the chaos that takes place when you
interrupt a trail of ants. Finally, Tony Thomas, one of our
producers, apologetically moved the guest to a place of
his own, and we all settled in. Laughing, Tony explained
that the show was successful, and we didn't want to break
our luck. That was with just a few of us . . . the same
holds true when we break for dinner and notes between
shows on taping day. This is served in a room upstairs, at
a very large U-shaped table, and now *all* the writers and
the support staff are there as well . . . some forty people . . . but no one ever switches places. We've made
the top ten in the ratings all season . . . we *like* where
we sit.

Paul Witt, another of our producers (aptly named, I
must say), grew a beard after "The Golden Girls" pilot,
while waiting to find out if the network was going to pick
up the show. They did, and he shaved. Now, we always
know when Witt/Thomas/Harris has another pilot show
in the works . . . Paul's whiskers begin to grow.

The seating situation was just habit with us, initially, before it grew into a superstition . . . which is probably how most good luck charms develop. Baseball players often go through a whole complicated routine when they step up to the plate . . . some, not all of it, can be attributed to signals involved in the game. The rest, however, is pure pandering to whatever baseball spirits might be lurking in the vicinity. "If I touch each corner of home plate with my bat, I'll be lucky!" In the beginning, he may have done that to settle himself down, but if he got a hit once or twice, habit quickly turns into superstition.

Some superstitions, like Paul's beard, are just good luck charms . . . plain and simple. When I was doing "The Pet Set," I always wore a cute little dog pin that Mom had given me for luck on the opening show. We did thirty-nine shows, and he was pinned on every one of them. We took a summer break, and somehow I misplaced him during the hiatus. The show wasn't picked up for the fall season. I found him again, months later, but by that time the horse was already stolen.

It isn't that I actually believe in superstition . . . it's all nonsense . . . but I wish people would stop telling me new ones. They stick in my mind.

If I leave the house, then have to come back in for something I forgot, I have to sit down and count to ten. Don't ask me why . . . I just have to. It was a tough sell with Allen, but I finally got him to do it, too. He'd sit there swearing . . . but counting.

If there is something I don't want to do, I will never

use sickness as an excuse, unless it is the truth . . . that's really pressing your luck.

If I drop a comb, I *must* step on it before I pick it up. This is not only stupid, it's unsanitary. But necessary.

If you pass me the salt, please don't think me rude if I don't take it from your hand . . . set it on the table and let me pick it up.

Never let me find knife blades lying across each other in the sink.

Putting a hat on the bed foretells a pregnancy. That one I've never given too much credence . . . if he puts his hat on the bed, he isn't staying long. A passing fancy.

Theater people, legitimate or otherwise, have the most colorful, understandably dramatic, and . . . I guess *weird* is the word I'm looking for . . . superstitions of all. The list is long and, I suspect, contingent upon geographic location, creativity of the people involved, and the success of the play in progress.

To get some specifics, I went to someone who has an ongoing romance with the theater . . . Estelle Getty. Lucky as we are to have her as Sophia, her first love is the Broadway stage . . . and the feeling is mutual. It was there that she won the Helen Hayes Award for *Torch Song Trilogy.*

Estelle says there are innumerable trivial theatrical superstitions . . . but here are the heavy numbers:

Never wear green. (My favorite color seems to get very bad press. Obviously, Mother Nature was never in the theater.)

Never whistle. I had always understood that you shouldn't whistle in the dressing room . . . Estelle says

NEVER! If you *do* whistle, you must walk outside, spit, turn around three times, then ask to be allowed back in . . . "Please, may I come in?" Boy, am I glad I didn't know about that one, all the times I sang "Whistle a Happy Tune" during *The King and I.* Maybe they just mean don't whistle *off*stage. I can't whistle anyway . . . the hell with it.

Never speak the name MacBeth backstage. As Estelle puts it, "Don't ever say the name of that Shakespearian King aloud!" As Gene Rayburn of "The Match Game" would put it . . . "King Blank."

So far, I have not heard of any superstitions specifically pertaining to television. Come to think of it, I spent my first five years in TV on Lucky Channel Thirteen. Maybe I'm exempt.

Knock wood.

On the Cosmic View

Use the word "cosmic" in casual conversation and watch people's eyes begin to glaze. It can have a somewhat pretentious flavor . . . especially coming out of someone who makes corny jokes . . . yet it is a word I use a lot in trying to explain my personal philosophy. (Talk about pretentious!)

"Cosmic view" is simply less of a mouthful than "keeping the overall picture in mind" . . . and it best describes an inner attitude I strive to maintain. Sometimes with more success than others. Describing an ephemeral outlook is next to impossible, maybe not even desirable . . . but, hey! . . . we've come this far together . . . let's have a go at it.

Day by day, we work our way through whatever is happening around us. I think of that as being at ground level . . . that's *now*. With the passage of time . . . a week, a month, a year . . . we begin to gain a little more perspective on this moment, and think of it as *then*. It's as though the camera is pulling back, ever so gradually. Finite details may begin to blur, but the picture keeps enlarging, taking in more and more. As the light changes, we see *now* in relationship with what has gone before. It begins to take on a pattern and, with any luck, even begins to make sense.

This overview is indispensable, it seems to me, to achieve any kind of objectivity. With practice, I find I can keep pulling that camera back just fine . . . unless I am personally involved. Then, of course, everything goes to hell in a handbasket.

A trivial, but typical, example of this overview concept is the fashion industry. Something is all the rage one minute, out the next, disappears momentarily, surfaces briefly as "high camp" in a comedy sketch, vanishes again, then sweeps back in as the height of today's "look." Joan Crawford's shoulder pads of the forties swept back in so far that we've started putting them in our underwear. No doubt they will be long gone before we go to press.

Now, when you have lived as long as I have, a pattern
in these cycles begins to emerge. You'd think it would be
possible to learn to predict them . . . unfortunately, my
hindsight is much better than my foresight, which needs
work.

Staying with fashion, but moving the camera back just
a little more, it's interesting to watch clothes come on
and off. Cave people didn't wear any at all until it turned
chilly. (We might forgive *them* for wearing fur, don't you
think?) And from then on the fun started.

Now, fast forward through history . . . more clothes,
less clothes, more, less, more . . . breasts are covered,
uncovered, covered . . . they're in, they're out . . .
sometimes they had to be out to be "in."

At this present moment in time, we keep showing a
little more skin each year, as the shock waves grow
smaller. At last, they cry, we are freeing ourselves from
the inhibitions of the past, and letting it all hang out.
Well, it's going to make me giggle when the big coverup
begins. We are about due for our friendly pendulum to
swing completely back the other way. We might even be
in for a spell of "demure." One can only hope they don't
resurrect the hoopskirt, designed to cover a Queen's
pregnancy. That could make a drastic change in "the
campus look."

To be sure, the cosmic view has its less frivolous side.
Keep in mind, there is no limit on how far back you can
pull the camera.

It has always fascinated me to realize that my mother,

born in 1899, saw the advent of so many things that we
take for granted as commonplace. So much more took
place in her eighty-seven years than did in her mother's
lifetime, or *her* mother's before *her* . . . automobiles,
planes, frozen foods, television, computers, a walk on
the moon, and space travel beyond!

The rate of forward movement, for better or worse,
continues to accelerate . . . more advances in less time.
A baby born this week has a considerably longer life
expectancy, all things being equal, than Mom's eighty-
seven years. Say he lives to be a hundred . . . he will see
the resolution of some of the problems with which we are
so preoccupied right now . . . he will have a progress
report on our other ongoing concerns . . . plus, he'll
see the beginnings of things you and I can't even imagine. Today's state-of-the-art hard- and software will be
archaic before he starts school!

All this can be an engrossing spectator sport, but as I
mentioned, one's objectivity is in direct proportion to his
degree of involvement. With all my efforts to keep my
perspective, there are certain issues on which my cosmic
approach goes out the window, and I'm right back at
ground level, joining the battle.

In my own lifetime (kid that I am!), it is easy to remember when we, the general public, thought of our planet in
terms of perpetuity. "Mother Earth" was indestructible.
Oceans were not considered, by the majority, to have a
fragile ecology . . . they had always been there, always
would be. Good air and pure water were taken for
granted as forever. Commercial foods were judged on

their flavor and convenience . . . their purity was sel-
dom questioned. Certain animal species and plant forms
went out of existence . . . completely and unnoticed.

In the last couple of decades, it has begun to dawn on
us that very real problems do exist in these areas . . .
that's a step in the right direction, at least, whether we as
individuals choose to *do* anything about them or not.

Looking ahead or looking back . . . I find them both
equally intriguing. It is not an either/or situation.

My father died twenty-five years ago, and just *think* of
what has come to pass since then . . . good and bad.
Horace White was a delightful free spirit, but I think that
if he were to come back today, and go to what would be
considered an average movie . . . even PG-rated . . .
he would be, shall we say . . . surprised. An ordinary
afternoon soap opera might blow his mind!

Allen has been gone only six years, but he, too, would
be in for a major culture shock . . . just at some of the
punchlines on "The Golden Girls" alone! To say nothing of seeing condoms advertised on television!

As our advances accelerate, so, too, do our problems
. . . and we have some corkers. Terrorism, world hun-
ger, crime, nuclear accidents, child abuse, the drug problem, AIDS, water and air pollution, overpopulation . . .
to name a few, in no particular order.

The doomsayers continue to throw up their hands and
proclaim that we are on our last hurrah as a human
species. "What does it all matter!" "The world is in such
a mess, anything goes!" They use this dogma to cover a

multitude of sins . . . and too many of these same individuals spend their lives on dead center.

I am not an ostrich. I read the papers . . . listen to the news. Even little Pollyanna here is forced to admit that it all does have an apocalyptic flavor. But dammit . . . I am going to continue to work as hard as I can in areas where I think I can help, and get on with my life! Otherwise . . . suppose I blow it all now, then, down the road, I look up to discover the sky hasn't fallen after all!

The doomsayers might be right, and my point of view, hopelessly naïve. Only time will tell . . . of which we may have a little or a lot. In the meantime, it does seem to me that theirs is a rather unrewarding philosophy, while we're waiting to find out.

No . . . I'm not an ostrich. Merely a cockeyed optimist.

On Fear

There are almost as many kinds of fear as there are varieties of love. Some are easy to understand, others are completely unreasonable. You start mentioning what you think of as your big fear . . . suddenly you find you have shaken the tree, and lots of little scary things come running out.

Introduce the word "fear," and I immediately think "fire." But what about spiders . . . most bugs, for that matter . . . stage fright, high places without hand railings, embarrassment? . . . I'd go on, but I'm afraid to.

Embarrassment is not unrelated to stage fright, come to think of it. Waiting to make an entrance onstage, your mouth dries up, you can't get your upper lip down off your front teeth, your heart is around your knees. Why? For fear of going out there and *embarrassing* yourself . . . and everyone else . . . by doing something really dumb. To be sure, this is not one of the more groundless fears . . . it has happened to me too often.

Does everybody get jittery before a show? Some admit it, others try to ignore it so it will go away, but I would bet that no one is completely immune. It also doesn't seem to matter how long you have been performing . . . while you may have a little more technique to fall back on, the panic is still there. Even lovely Helen Hayes told me one time that she gets physically ill before a show.

Someone should put a camera on the four Golden Girls before showtime some Friday night. We gather in a tiny area offstage by the living room set, waiting to be introduced to the studio audience. Rue McClanahan, "Blanche," will look you in the eye and swear she never gets stage fright. She is *excited* before a show, she says, but not nervous. Well . . . then I guess I've seen her when she's been pretty excited! Bea, "Dorothy," gets very quiet, and about four inches taller . . . when she grabs your hand, you can hear the bones crack. Estelle Getty, "Sophia," talks about retiring to her sister's condominium in Florida and getting out of show business . . . she doesn't mean later in life, she's talking about right *then!* As far as "Rose" is concerned, I feel myself getting aggressively cheerful, whipping up the spirits of the troops. Unable to stop myself, all I need is a letter sweater and pompoms . . . one night all three of those ladies are going to deck me.

Stage fright is not a show business exclusive . . . we just abuse the privilege. It is there for everyone who walks into a new job, a new date, new in-laws . . . even walking into a party can be agony for someone who is not socially oriented. Butterflies, as beautiful as they are, should stay in the garden where they belong.

Wonder who first described that awful feeling of terror as "having butterflies"? It's such a misnomer . . . butterflies make you feel good just looking at them, even if they can't fly without staggering.

It's difficult to equate butterflies with bugs . . . they are the privileged class of the insect family.

Other insects don't really make me feel warm all over. Spiders, in particular, were a basic phobia for most of my life . . . I couldn't look at them without that cold chill running all through my body. I really worked at overcoming this nonsense, and tried to concentrate on all the good they do . . . but I would still turn to Jell-O when one would drop in front of me. They *know* this! Let there be one spider in a room full of people, and he'll find me. Whether he is poisonous or not is of no consequence . . . even a poor old daddy longlegs could get to me . . . until a very few years ago . . . a friend gave me a copy of *Charlotte's Web*, and I began to shape up. Today I can even coax a spider into a jar to take him outside to

release him. Once that is accomplished . . . *then* I have
my shuddering fit. I'm getting better.

It is short-sighted to badmouth the world of insects
. . . I even feel they might resent being called "bugs."
They are truly remarkable when you think about it.
Three fourths of all known animal species are insects.
They have inhabited the world for three hundred and
seventy-five million years . . . there are over one mil-
lion species . . . and *only one tenth of one percent* of the
whole gang can be termed pests.

That's not the half of it. The average insect weighs one
ten-thousandth of an ounce . . . yet all the insects on
earth put together weigh twelve times as much as the
human population! Most of all, I would like to meet the
fellow who figured all that up.

These could be a few of the reasons that so many of us
are intimidated by these creatures. Plus the fact that long
after humans have disappeared . . . they will still be
around.

My good friend Beatrice Arthur has a weak spot or two
herself. Bea loves animals and gives a tremendous
amount on their behalf. However one day on "The
Golden Girls" our script revolved around a piano-play-
ing chicken. Naturally, I for one was delighted that we
were getting to work with a live creature. For the first two
days we rehearsed with a toy . . . the star chicken
wasn't called in until Wednesday. Came the big day, and
when "Count Bessie" arrived on the set, Bea turned pale
as a ghost . . . and split! Poor darling, she hadn't said
anything, but she has a terrible phobia about live chick-

ens . . . *all* live chickens, not just ones that play the
piano. Since we had several scenes to play together, they
had to be staged so that Bea was on one side of the room,
and "Bessie" and Betty were as far from her as possible.

Bea is not alone in this phobia . . . Alfred Hitchcock
made a very lucrative film about it called *The Birds.* It just
came as a surprise to us to see what it did to Bea, who
always seems to be in control of any situation. We were
all very understanding and sympathetic. Of course, Rue
and Estelle and I will never tease her about it. Nor will we
make a lot of ongoing chicken jokes from here on out. Of
course we won't. Certainly not.

As I said in the beginning, my real bête noir is fire. Not
the cozy kind in a stone fireplace, when you're cuddled
up with a cold drink and a warm friend . . . or at least a
good book. That is civilized domesticated fire. I'm talking about the wild variety . . . *Fire!* It scares everyone,
or at least it should, but I'm talking sheer paralyzing
panic.

Living in California almost all my life, and seeing what
havoc a brushfire can wreak, probably accounts for a
good part of my terror. Or it may have stemmed from
one of my earliest recollections . . . being camped out
in the High Sierras with my folks, and seeing a forest fire
creeping over the ridge just beyond us. I shall never
forget the terrified animals crashing through the brush
ahead of the fire . . . deer, squirrels, snakes, chipmunks
. . . even a porcupine. Dad broke camp in short order,
and he and Mom got us packed up and *out.* I can still
remember running with a can of evaporated milk, thinking I was helping. To this day, when I see a pall of smoke

in the sky indicating a brushfire, I revert right back to the little kid with the tin can.

Seeing someone toss a burning cigarette out of a car is enough to make me absolutely paranoid.

I don't even want to think about what happens to Bea if she passes a poultry truck.

On Other Fears

My list of fears keeps growing until I begin to wonder if I have always been chicken. (Sorry, Bea!)

Although something of a tomboy, I managed to get through growing up without any broken bones. I worked hard at capture the flag, king of the mountain, and kick the can, logged a *lot* of hours on the rings and horizontal bars, and skated thousands of miles dreaming of joining the Ice Follies . . . but I lacked the fearlessness that must be in every true competitor. I would practice a back somersault off the high bar . . . sometimes it even worked . . . but it *always* hurt. Not giving it that extra push was probably what got me through relatively un-scathed . . . Mary Lou Retton I wasn't.

As I grew a little older, I also managed to get through without any broken hearts, during the years when that is usually par for the course. Again, it was because I was afraid of pain, I guess. I would do one of two things . . . either worship someone from a nice safe anonymous

distance (Arnie Ballantyne, who was our high school stu-
dent body president, is a good for instance) . . . or, if I
was going out with someone, be prepared to run if I so
much as imagined he showed a flicker of interest elsewhere.

Fortunately, I learned you can't live your whole life
that way. Through the intervening years I haven't always
kept my guard up, and I have the bruises to prove it.

Today, with Allen gone, every interview includes the
question "Do you think you will ever marry again?" and
my honest answer is a firm "No!" The main and really
only reason for this is because Allen and I had such a
great time, it would be tough . . . no, impossible . . .
ever to make a complete commitment again.

Way in the back of my mind, however, a nagging little
question pops up . . . could it also be fear? Fear that, at
this late date, someone might want me today, but lose
interest down the road a piece? (So to speak.) Fear that
having adjusted to living alone . . . and really treasur-
ing the privacy . . . that I would find myself unable to
fully share my life on a twenty-four-hour-a-day basis
again? Fear that involuntary comparisons . . . (not only
my memories of Allen, but my new partner would have
ghosts of his own) . . . would prove more than we
could handle?

Mind you, I don't lose sleep wondering about any of
these things. But since we were talking about my being
somewhat chicken as a kid, it occurred to me . . .
wouldn't it be funny if I was now reverting to childhood,
and playing it safe once again? Funny peculiar, that is
. . . not funny ha-ha.

Some of the minor fears that are ever-present when you live alone are very down-to-earth and unglamorous . . . the little routine things that you could always check out with your husband. Did I put too much rouge on? Is my breath okay? Does my hair cover my head, or does that little pink spot show? (We called it "checking the hole in my head.") Do I snore? Allen swore that I didn't, and we had a covenant to be brutally honest about such things . . . all I can do is hope I still don't, because the dogs aren't going to tell me.

Then there are the big fears.

Fear of doing something stupid, like tripping on a rug, or falling downstairs, and not being able to call anybody. We used to call my father "the Hummingbird" because he had a tendency to charge around at top speed. I do the same, and being a card-carrying klutz, I bump into things a lot. When I am alone in the house, I try to remember to slow down a little, and not carry six things when I'm heading downstairs. At least it is an effort toward common sense . . . beyond that, I refuse to fret about it.

And the deep fears.

Fear of death is not one of my problems . . . only of the dying. The *how*, not the *when* of it. Getting there is not half the fun, and the fear of doing it badly could be of concern if I wanted to waste time thinking about it. I

don't. I figure I will improvise when the time comes . . .
some things are better without rehearsal.

Death . . . the one sure thing that every creature on
earth shares in common . . . is still such a personal
matter. Each of us has a different approach to it, and a
different perception when, or if, we think about it.

At a distance . . . a natural disaster, a far-off war, an
epidemic, a famine . . . death is a grim but remote sta-
tistic. Closer to home . . . murder reports, traffic casu-
alties, the passing of someone of note . . . it captures
our attention momentarily. Not until it strikes someone
near to us does death become a tangible reality, and this
is where we all separate into our individual attitudes.

My earliest experience with what being dead meant
was in the loss of a beloved pet. My folks handled it in
such a sensitive way that it made the loss of my grand-
mother, shortly after, a little easier to comprehend. I was
led to understand that all the grief was left on our side, to
handle the best we could out of our love for her . . . but
Grandma was free, and she now *knew* what we could only
wonder about.

Simplistic as it sounds, this approach really took any
fear of death itself completely away. I still want to make
the most, and the best, of the time here, but then I know
there is one more adventure coming up . . . one big
mystery to be solved. So many times through the years,
when we'd hear of someone going, Mom and I would say
to each other, "He knows the secret." And now she
knows it, too.

For centuries, comedy has had a close affiliation with
death. How often, figuratively, has the tragedy death

mask been turned upside down for laughs? The same holds true to this day.

If a comic does a bit that really works, "He killed 'em!" . . . If it *doesn't* get the laughs, "He died out there!"

"You slay me!" is a compliment.

"I died laughing!" is another one.

To describe an audience's overall reaction, it is either a "live" house or a "dead" one.

Maybe that is whistling through the graveyard . . . to show lack of fear. Perhaps it has something to do with superstition. The ancient Chinese would begin to worry if things seemed to be going too well, and shaking a fist to heaven, would cry, "Bad rice! Bad rice!" . . . in an attempt to hide the good fortune from the gods, lest it be taken away.

This is about as heavy as we're going to get. Probably this piece won't ever make the book . . . but I enjoyed exploring a path I rarely travel, and have no idea where it leads. I'll be dying to find out.

On Moods

In spite of all the wheezing away that I do about trying to maintain a positive attitude, I am forced to admit that we are all subject to extreme mood swings. Sometimes we handle them . . . sometimes they handle us.

The color chart of moods always intrigues me. Red
with anger . . . purple with rage . . . green with envy
. . . white with fear . . . in a black mood . . . a case of
the blues . . . the coward is yellow. Plus all the shades
in between. Blanche, on "The Golden Girls," referred to
a really bad time as "one of those magenta days."

No one ever seems to describe a really *good* mood in
terms of a color . . . at least none that I can think of
offhand. Looking at the world through rose-colored
glasses, maybe? In the pink? Everything's peachy?

Our lives are said to be a series of cycles . . . little
ones within big ones, an up cycle versus a down cycle
. . . which accounts for the spells of euphoria, as well as
the blahs. Learning to use the one and defeat the other
would make us into very productive individuals . . . but
those who can manage that balancing act are few and far
between.

I'm not sure I would want to be *that* in control. It
sounds a little bloodless. How would you appreciate the
really high spots with nothing to measure them against?
It's comforting to know that's *one* worry I don't have to
spend time on.

There are days when I feel I can accomplish almost
anything I tackle. I fly from one task to the next with no
wasted motion (at least that's what I like to *picture* myself
doing), while my mind is planning two steps ahead. My
energy is boundless . . . and my judgment is so faulty
that I manage to believe it is always this way. I completely
forget the inevitable doldrums sure to be upcoming,
when doing *anything* is like pushing a car uphill with a wet

rope. I'm not tired, or ill . . . I simply can't get it in gear.

Unfortunately, all those things to which I said, "Sure I will," when I was in my Wonder Woman mode, are now on the schedule . . . while my mind and energy are suddenly out to lunch!

These are the times to beware. Having to push, nothing goes right, and I make dumb mistakes. Knowing it's all my fault to begin with only increases the frustration and inefficiency. It isn't long before the demon Depression sees a chance to move in, and I have to battle it out. My most effective defense is to become so involved with trying to get everything done, that I don't have time to be depressed.

However, on occasion . . . rarely for me, thank God . . . the battle turns into hand-to-hand combat. Busyness no longer works, and for no apparent reason, the candle snuffer begins to lower over my head. Sometimes it's a sudden feeling that washes over like a wave . . . even when things *should* be the best. Try as I will to move on and away from it, the feeling keeps pace with me.

Once in a great while, it becomes imperative to turn around and confront the monster. I have learned the hard way that if I *don't* do this, it will keep eating away at me until real damage is done. I know the time has come to get very quiet and try to listen for what is actually bothering me. It takes an amount of digging . . . sometimes I even come up with some surprises . . . but it can be done. By identifying whatever is really bugging me, and bringing it into the light, it begins to lose its clout, and may eventually evaporate altogether.

Deep Depression . . . the genuine article . . . is

something else. It is acute and agonizing, and far beyond a simple home remedy . . . so devastating that outside help is usually needed.

What I try and do is shore up my defenses against ever getting to that point. Recognizing the enemy *early* in the fight is an advantage. Mood highs and lows are normal, but if I let myself settle into a pattern of too many lows, it can easily slip over into feeling sorry for myself. The enemy thrives on self-indulgence, and I'm damned if I'm going to provide him with a breeding ground.

Then there are the bright days (whatever we choose to color them) when euphoria strikes . . . equally unbidden. It bubbles up inside with such a feeling of excitement . . . it's what makes Snoopy go into his silly dance . . . it's what some call spring fever, whatever the time of year . . . it's what Mom and I used to know as "that Good Feeling," almost like a premonition of something great about to happen. It's pure unadulterated JOY is what it is. Greet it when it comes and don't ask questions . . . it doesn't stick around long.

Somewhere between the two extreme mood swings is where we all spend most of our time. With a little effort, we can make the territory as livable as possible.

Beverly Sills's mother was being interviewed one time about her famous opera star daughter, and I have always loved her response to a question about Beverly's life offstage. She said, "Beverly isn't always happy, but she's always cheerful." It's a good point of view, and makes life a lot more pleasant . . . hopefully for Beverly, but certainly for a lot of other people.

There are those . . . more than a few . . . to whom
cheerfulness is absolutely infuriating. When their long
faces become too obvious to ignore, you ask, "Is anything wrong?" "Not a thing. I'm just in a bad mood."
Now I find *that* infuriating! To each his'n.

Mind over matter. For me it works. As a case in point, I
am never troubled by jet lag on a cross-continental flight
. . . I simply leave my watch on California time, and my
body is none the wiser. With Allen, however, jet lag
would really wipe him out. I could never understand why
it was a problem for him whether he was going east and
losing three hours, or heading west where he *gained* three
hours. To him it made perfect sense. Jet lag was something you got on an airplane!

Perhaps I am merely psyching myself out about all this
mood business, but just let me be. I'm happy and harmless. Maybe the reason I don't feel my age could be that I
never reset my calendar either.

On Aging

For those who live to tell about it.

One of my mother's close friends would always excuse
anything she did with "I'm old enough to be eccentric."

She and Mom were in their seventies when they met,

yet I always had the distinct impression that this lady had been saying that since puberty.

There are people like that. Even as kids, they do things *their* way, and somehow manage to carry it off. They aren't exactly leaders . . . but they sure as hell aren't followers. Eccentric.

We've all known them.

I remember one . . . a girl at school, Carey Wilson. Her hair was long and all frizzed out. Sounds like the height of fashion today, but at that point in time, we . . . her classmates . . . thought it bordered on weird. To complete the picture, she would set a little black velvet beret on top of all that hair, then come to *school!* Mind you, this was at the age when the rest of us were spending every ounce of energy and allowance on being clones of each other. God forbid we should get caught looking *different!* Sleeping on rollers was a way of life.

Secretly, I'm sure we all admired Carey's independence. I, for one, spent a lot of time wondering how she kept her hat up there, and why it didn't mash her hair down . . . but I don't remember anyone ever trying to copy her. One guy in chemistry class, maybe.

And I'm sure it wasn't deliberate on Carey's part. She was not one of those who work so hard at "being different" they practically glow in the dark. She was a genuine original.

Wonder what ever happened to Carey. Something interesting, I'll bet.

Look at some of the people we know today. Don't you sometimes wonder what they were like at that age? Carol Channing, for instance. She is the original's original . . . but how, or when, did she get that way?

Carol cannot have been an ordinary child. She and I
have been great and good friends for twenty-five years.
Her husband and mine go back even further. Charles
Lowe and Allen Ludden served together in World War II.

Once I asked Charles what Carol's childhood was like
. . . before eyelashes. He told me she lived in San Fran-
cisco, was brought up in Christian Science, and when she
was four she took part in a show at a nearby little theater.
According to Charlie, "She walked on stage at four and
never got off!"

Carol has always been larger than life. It is almost as if
someone had sketched her, then animated the result. It's
interesting that Carol and Charlie's son Channing Lowe
is a fine cartoonist with the Fort Lauderdale *Sun-Sentinel.*

Carol has never missed a performance to my knowledge . . . even turning a broken arm to advantage. She
got so much mileage out of doing *Jerry's Girls* in a cast, I
accused her of breaking the arm on purpose. Her days off
are happily booked to accommodate extra jobs in addition to whatever show she is doing. As a workaholic, she
puts me in the shade.

It all must agree with her. Under all the wigs and the
makeup, Carol is one of the most serene people I know.
Wouldn't it be funny if she was once somebody's Carey
Wilson?

People like that you remember. Like it or not, they are
interesting. They don't have to spend years of seasoning
like the rest of us to garner some individuality . . . if,
indeed, we ever do.

It is my firm conviction that while time is wreaking its
havoc on the *outside* of us, the person *inside* doesn't

change all that much. The years may mellow the forceful individual, or, with any luck, bring a little assurance to the timid soul . . . but underneath all the silt of experience that settles is the same personality that was there in the beginning. Stir up the silt every now and then and watch that same personality shoot for the surface.

It is a fascinating phenomenon to watch for . . . in yourself as well as in others. You'll know it when you see it. The fun of this private little game is that it not only makes you more sensitive to the people around you . . . it keeps you so tuned in you forget to grow old.

Age has become one of the major preoccupations of our society. If the same is true in other cultures, we are in even bigger trouble than I suspected . . . not as Americans . . . as human beings. But let's not borrow trouble. That is another whole book for someone else to write.

In the meantime, for those in the job market here, age goes deeper than mere vanity. For men as well as women . . . livelihoods can be at risk.

Any television show done in front of a studio audience in Hollywood has a warm-up announcer whose job it is to loosen everyone up to enjoy the show. Whether it is a situation comedy, talk show, game show . . . no matter what . . . one of the first questions that announcer will be asked is "How old is so-and-so?"

At an award dinner recently, my dinner partner was not only beautiful, but a delightful conversationalist. More importantly, she was a hard-working charity volunteer, and a major donor as well. With all this going for this lovely lady . . . her first question, as each celebrity approached the microphone, was "How old do you think . . . etc., etc." . . . How unnecessarily sad.

Of late there has been a growing awareness of "the graying of America" . . . brought on by recent statistics . . . and it seems to be in a positive sense. If that were not the case, a show such as "The Golden Girls" wouldn't stand a chance . . . again art is imitating life. I am delighted to see even a tendency in that direction, but the old Cosmic View leads me to be cautious. I just hope it isn't the new "in" thing, temporarily current and choice. Maybe if it stays around long enough we'll stop counting, and judge others on merit.

Remember Carol Burnett's question-and-answer session . . . and how inventive she could be when the age question invariably arose?

Anyhow . . . "growing old" is a contradiction in terms.

Wouldn't it be better to grow smart?
So many otherwise healthy people are on a collision course with old age. They literally *wait* for it to catch up.
The dread starts early on:
"I can't believe it. I'm going to be thirty!"
"It's all over. I'll soon be forty."
"My God! Fifty!!"
These poor souls take all the bloom off of the last half of each decade, dreading the next big number.
My mother, bless her, would never hold still for that

attitude, nor would she tolerate it in others. For one thing, she considered it to be the height of ingratitude for all the good stuff. This outlook kept her spirit polished so brightly that it sustained her through the last three painful years when her body let her down.

It took Allen a while to really believe that his two White girls truly didn't concern themselves with the *number* of years.

When my forty-ninth birthday rolled around, he devised an elaborately wonderful surprise party that really worked. Somehow, without my having a clue, he managed to get forty-nine good friends together and marched me into the most complete surprise of my life. In a funny, touching toast, he explained that he was hoping to soften the edge of the Big One coming up next year.

The upshot, of course, was that when the next year rolled around, he was stuck with another party to *celebrate* "The Big One."

And it will be ever thus as far as I am concerned. I don't want to *fight* old age, but I'm not about to invite it to live in, either. I want a nice symbiotic relationship with it, where we are totally unaware of each other.

If this sounds strange . . . remember, I'm old enough to be eccentric.

On Aging . . . P.S.

There is one area in which age *does* concern me . . . that is in regard to my beloved four-legged Superfriends. It has been my great and good fortune to have had many of these guys around for a long, full life . . . in their terms.

BOOTIE	*Pekingese*	15 years
BINKY	*Pekingese*	12
SIMBA	*Pekingese*	11
BANDIT	*Pekingese*	15
DANCER	*Poodle*	13
STORMY	*St. Bernard*	11
WILLIE	*Poodle*	14
EMMA	*Poodle*	13
NICKY	*Poodle*	almost 17
SOONER	*Lab/Golden Retriever*	15½

That's a pretty fair record. And every one of those years represents total mutual joy, no matter what else was going on in my life at the time. It's difficult to make such an unequivocal statement about even your closest and dearest two-legged friends.

Having read each other's body language for so long, you notice when your pal begins to slow up a little, and you become aware of a certain weariness . . . the years are catching up. It's a time to be extra considerate and

tuned in. As with anyone you love, this is when you make
the most of the time left . . . you don't take it for
granted, but grow closer than ever if such a thing is
possible.

For anyone to whom pets are important family members, it is a heartache that they have a shorter road to
travel than we do. But we knew that going in. If I were to
pro rate the grief I have felt, each time I lose one of these
friends, against the pleasure and comfort they dished out
through their stay with me . . . it's no contest. The
grief is a fair price to pay.

Our lives together rarely come out even . . . that just
isn't the nature of things. Sometimes an older person
who loses a pet has the feeling that there aren't enough
years left to commit to a new puppy or kitten. In this
case, the human road may be the shorter one . . . and
the thought of giving up animals completely only compounds the unhappiness over the loss of their pet.

There is one solution to this dilemma that I have seen
work wonders, again and again. Every shelter has a ros-
ter of fine, healthy older dogs and cats. They are not
senior citizens, by any means, but they are far enough
past puppydom and kittenhood to minimize their
chances for adoption.

These animals are over the rambunctiousness of
youth, settled in their ways, and have some very good
years to go. They need a friend, desperately, and their
gratitude is boundless . . . they will adapt themselves to
whatever is required. It may sound like wishful thinking

. . . I would think so, too, if I hadn't seen it happen so
many times.

Old friends *can* be the best friends. Anybody knows
that.

IV

OFF MY CHEST

On Things I Hate

Sure, I'm a cockeyed optimist.

If the truth were known, it no doubt stems from trying to compensate for a lifelong tendency to be hypercritical. I probably overdo it, giving the impression that I think *everything* is simply peachy, and wouldn't let a negative thought enter my flowery, pointed little head.

Au contraire. Oh, how very contraire!!

As there is a lengthy list of things that drive me straight up the wall, let's get some of them out of my system right now.

These are a few of my unfavorite things:

For openers, I hate the word "hate," but let's call 'em as we see 'em.

I hate making decisions. Big or small, I agonize over them . . . even when there is a clear-cut choice. Bless the man who *tells* me where we are going and what we are going to do. (For the record, this craven indecision holds true only up to a given hour.)

I hate people who take their half out of the middle. Whether it's in an automobile, pushing a market basket, or simply walking down the sidewalk . . . it says a lot about them. Look at their faces. The expressions are identical to the sheep you sometimes encounter on a country road. They are going to cross, no matter what, and it's up to *you* to avoid *them.* It isn't really rudeness . . . as far as they are concerned, you don't exist.

Those people must be kin to the ones who move in too close, physically . . . invading that little bubble of space we all have that is our own. If I'm waiting in line, or standing in casual conversation, let someone crowd nearer than necessary, and I begin to squirm. It may be only a matter of inches, but it's important. With animals it's called "critical distance," and it's different for each individual . . . but cross that line and the animal takes flight. I can empathize.

Of course, we are not speaking of a romantic encounter . . . in which case all bets are off. For damn sure.

I hate loud noises . . . with the possible exception of thunder, which, I reluctantly admit, I find exciting, but only if it doesn't spook my dogs. Fireworks make me furious except at great distance . . . seen and not heard. And professionally supervised, *please!*

I hate the word "bored" or any of its derivatives.

I hate the expression "lonely only child." It is so often specious . . . but more on that later.

I hate bathroom humor. Scatology is a real turnoff, and it would be fine with me if bodily functions stayed in the closet (figuratively, not literally). Conversely, I like light touch doubl' entendre. I get tickled by things that say one thing but can also mean something quite different. The fun of it is . . . it's harmless. Those who don't

get it can take the first meaning and go happily on their
way, while the more depraved of us can enjoy a good
laugh at no one's expense. But be sure to laugh and *move
on*. Deliver me from the heavy-handed leerer who is so
afraid the second meaning might escape that he belabors
the poor thing right into the ground. By this time you
wish you'd stayed home. Why is it that some people can
say almost anything without offending . . . while others
can make "Raspberries!" sound dirty? Attitude, I guess.

I hate snide sarcasm. There is a certain patronizing
tone of voice that can instantly set my teeth on edge.

I hate sloppy diction. Words were invented for communication, which is tough enough at best   Mum-
bling only compounds the problem. Some television
commercials seem bent on eliminating certain conso
nants:

"This soap is gen-le on your hands '
"Call your frien'ly travel agent."

Genuine regional accents *are* forgiven.
Don't let your mouth *or* your pen mumble. If you have
a difficult name, for instance, help other people by saying
and writing it clearly . . . be proud of it. Admittedly,
some of the world's greatest have had execrable handwriting, which makes a complete bum of my argument. I
really hate that!

I hate having to put the shades down on an airplane
just at sunset time so they can run the movie. But I know

how to get even . . . I put my shades down, yes, but I don't watch the damned film! That'll show 'em!

I hate wrinkles.

On my face. On my body. In my clothes.

Think of all the effort that went into inventing new miracle fabrics that don't wrinkle . . . then some genius decides they aren't chic! As a result, you put your clothes on, feel crisp and fresh for about twenty seconds . . . sit down one time, and you get up looking like an unmade bed.

As a result, the crumpled look is *in.* We're right back where we started, with pure linen and pongee . . . both of which look wonderful . . . on the hanger.

I still like to at least start smooth . . . but, of course, anything can be carried to extremes . . . I do feel a little foolish when I catch myself pressing a sweat shirt before I put it on.

The only place wrinkles look good is on a Shar-Pei puppy.

George Burns is militantly antiwrinkle. When he's working he doesn't put his pants on until the very last minute before he goes on stage, so there won't be any sitting wrinkles . . . it's his old vaudeville training. I feel I'm in good company . . . if anyone thinks I'm too fussy, I can always say, "What's good enough for George Burns is good enough for me!"

I hate whiners.

I hate onions.

I hate those sunglasses that are like mirrors, so you see yourself instead of someone's eyes.

And the list goes on . . .

I'm sure you care.

On Being Only

"So, you're an only child. Aw, poor baby!"

If not those exact words, the implied pity has a familiar ring to it. This attitude is such a common one that it has not only been generally accepted, but perpetuated.

It is true that my personal reaction is anything but objective, but I take great pleasure in shooting down such drivel whenever the opportunity presents itself. "Only" and "lonely" are rhymes . . . not synonyms.

Like all sweeping generalizations, the idea that because a child grows up without sibling support and/or rivalry, he is inevitably doomed to be either a lonely little waif, a selfish spoiled brat, or both is absolutely specious. The fact that some only children *do* fulfill the prophecy can be chalked up to the law of averages.

It isn't because a child has no brothers or sisters that he turns into a monster . . . it is how his parents *handled* the situation. We've all known any number of selfish, spoiled, lonely little waifs who were surrounded by brothers and sisters. So much depends on whether the parents were doting on the youngest, favoring the first-born, or giving short shrift to someone in the middle. Each case is a custom situation, and blanket assumptions don't work.

Let's forget negatives for a minute, and talk about

some of the good stuff that comes with the territory of being an only child. I must stick with personal experience only, or I can find myself guilty of those same sweeping generalizations. Let's just say it worked great for me.

Having one child was not a considered decision on the part of my folks. A month before I was born, my mother was in a bad car accident, and the doctors were forced to patch up her skull fracture before they could worry about the baby. I managed to hang in there, but the question of more children was, by then, academic.

Far from being lonely, I always had all the friends of my own age I could ask for. They were made very welcome at our house when I invited them . . . but having them there was my *choice* . . . I wasn't stuck with them, like it or not, because we happened to be related.

The biggest plus, of course, was the special relationship that existed between my parents and me. We were buddies . . . a solid threesome through good times and bad. We had fun together, laughed a lot, always had some silly game going . . . but my mom and dad also ran a very tight ship. "No" meant "no," not "maybe" or "I don't think so." The word was never used lightly. I caught on very early that when I heard "no" it was a waste of time to pursue the subject, and I would move on to something with more potential.

Sure, I was doted on and indulged, when we could afford it . . . remember, I was the only game in town! But I was never, repeat *never*, allowed to take it for granted as my due. If at any time I showed signs of beginning to believe my own publicity, there was hell to pay, and it was made abundantly clear that things were only worthwhile and attainable if they were appreciated. That has held me in good stead all my life. Sharing was the way it was at our house . . . only they called it "keeping things in balance."

With just the three of us, I had no live-in peer group with whom to gang up. I was spared the "us against them" syndrome, and could enjoy adults, as well as friends my own age. Rather than thinking of grown-ups as something to tolerate or be bored by, I found that many of them weren't half bad . . . even if they *were* taller.

My favorite tall person was my mother's brother Tom. He was my hero, I was his slave. In reality, Uncle Tom was seven years younger than my mother, but to me he was my absolute contemporary. He could fix anything . . . or tease me unmercifully without hurting. He taught me to play poker when I was six, and to drive a car when I was sixteen. He told me those were the *only* two things he never wanted to catch me doing like a woman.

In their wisdom, neither my folks nor Tom ever talked down to me. From the time I can remember, a conversation was never scaled down for my benefit . . . if I didn't get all of it, that was my problem. Questions were answered, but I was not center stage.

It was the same in the humor department. We all loved jokes, and my dad, being a traveling man with a delicious sense of humor, always had a good supply. Once in a while he would add a word of caution. "Now, that one we don't take to school, honey." The only rule about a joke

was it had to be funny. If it was a little raunchy in the
bargain, it had better be *really* funny enough to justify it.
Merely *dirty* jokes didn't qualify.

There was no such thing as "man's work" and "woman's work" at home that I can ever recall. Everybody
would pitch in at whatever needed doing. Evidently, I
was always busy doing something else when cooking
time rolled around. My repertoire in that department is
limited.

Vacations were the highlights of each year . . . better
even than Christmas. The three of us nature nuts would
have a glorious time investigating this lovely planet together . . . again something that has proven a constant
source of wonder and joy to this day.

Perhaps I am looking back with rose-colored hindsight, but that really is the way I remember it. For me,
being an only child was something wonderful.

Oddly enough, three of my very closest friends over
the past many many years are also only children. Although our growing up years were all totally different,
geographically, economically, whatever . . . we all
agree that being a single child was not half bad.

Being an only *adult*, however, can be something else.

The family closeness that I treasured was not easy for
other people I cared about to really believe . . . much
less understand. The men in my life especially. More
than once there would be jealousy to contend with, and it
would be tough to handle . . . jealousy probably on

both sides . . . but since I was in the middle, I am not what you might call an objective judge.

Also, when you are one in number, in times of emergency, there is no one to fill in for you. You find yourself trying desperately to split your loyalties in order to cover all the bases . . . and, as a result, you wind up spreading yourself so thin, you don't do full justice to anybody.

That is only one example of why I am eternally grateful for God's great sense of timing. It carried me through the two toughest periods of my life.

During my husband's long and hopeless illness, my mother was well and fit, not only able to take care of herself, but to help me in so many ways . . . including leaving me free to make the most of every precious moment with Allen.

Mom was there when I needed her . . . to do all of those practical little daily things that are always necessary, no matter what else is going on. The rest of the time she would busy herself elsewhere, . . . which kept me from ever getting the feeling that I was neglecting her.

Toward the end, when Allen remained in the hospital, Mom stayed at my house. When I'd come in from being with Allen, she would meet me with something refreshing . . . then give me time to sort myself out. She never hit me as I came in the door, with all those obvious questions to which she knew there were no answers. She waited . . . and let me volunteer my meager report when I was ready.

I wonder if I ever told her how much I appreciated that.

By the time Mom's last long three-year challenge came, Allen was no longer here. I was able to concentrate on her completely, keeping her with me where we could enjoy the good time together. Had the order been reversed, I would have wound up short-changing one or the other or both of them. And if you are an only adult, that can tear you apart.

As God knows, better than anyone . . . timing is everything.

On Writing It Down

Much as I love them, words do get in the way sometimes. That is one of the reasons I love listening to music with my cat and dogs . . . they don't keep talking all through it, telling me how beautiful it is.

The spoken word can also get you in a whole lot of trouble. If a point is interrupted before it is made, the meaning can be changed completely, and the original intent garbled beyond recognition. Yet, in a heated discussion, who has not been guilty of jumping into someone else's sentence?

My mother had a way around this. When there was something important she wanted to discuss, but knew it was a potentially incendiary issue, she would write it down in the form of a note . . . sometimes a letter . . . and leave it for me to find when I was alone. She was a very articulate lady . . . even more so on paper. This way I had a chance to digest what she had to say, and think about my response, instead of answering off the top of my head. *Then* we would talk about it. If it was a clear-cut case of my doing something wrong, I would even be able to write out an explanation, or apology, and leave it for *her* to find . . . if everything had been said that was necessary, we would move on. So often, in a confrontation, you keep repeating the same things . . . plowing the same tired field, over and over, without really resolving anything. Especially with two big talkers . . . which we were.

Needless to say, Mom and I didn't abuse this privilege . . . it would have lost its punch. We only used it for something vitally important. I still think it was a good idea . . . and I can tell you, when I would come home to find one of those envelopes, in that pretty handwriting, it got my attention!

That probably accounts for the fact that, to this day, there are times when the urge to get something out of my system by writing it down, is irresistible. For just such times as these, I keep a Special Drawer.

If I have gone to the trouble of putting something down on paper, I keep it, at least overnight. My private rule is, I look at it again the next morning . . . if I still feel the same, it goes into "The Drawer." If it is absolute *garbahj*, it is broomed at that point. This gets rid of at least half.

The way the game works, once in "The Drawer," the stuff is never rewritten, as that would eradicate what the feeling was at the moment. It would be like removing fingerprints from the scene of the crime.

Every so often . . . even a few years can sneak by
. . . it is interesting to read through these heavy numbers from a different perspective. Now, these I don't cull.
I figure if they have made it this far, they deserve a
permanent home . . . so they go into "The Box," high
on a shelf.

Perhaps I'm hoping they'll breed.

Perhaps it's as well that they don't.

Putting it in writing while the heat is still on is a wonderful way of venting temper privately. For those occasions when you know if you lose it you'll get in nothing
but trouble, it's a lifesaver. It also tends to keep you from
storing up for a future disaster.

What brought this up? I found a couple of pages recently, at the bottom of "The Drawer" . . . (obviously,
it doesn't fill up too fast) . . . that were scribbled one
night, a few years back, following a heated discussion.

Our son David and his wife Kathleen were visiting, and
Sarah, our youngest, was still living at home. I can remember where we were sitting, what we were wearing
. . . practically even what we'd had for dinner . . . I
just don't remember the subject we were discussing. Minor detail. The following is an excerpt from two pages
that I had written later that night . . . obviously still in
temper.

"I have no platform from which to speak. I am uninformed. I am not really very bright. Granted, I am very
emotional. But I am no more uninformed than those
who are sounding off the loudest. I am every bit as

bright, by nature, and certainly a *lot* wiser by experience, than some of the loud voices of authority to which I have been subjected of late. And as for being emotional . . . we are suddenly in a whole new dimension in this type of exchange, where emotion equates with violence, sanity equates with '*I* think,' and judgment equates with really nothing at all!"

Well!!! I hope I felt better after that outburst. Glad nobody saw it. It sure could use a rewrite.

The point is, however, I didn't (hopefully) say it where it would have thrown more fuel on what was already a pretty good fire. It must also be remembered that I was, in fact, a protagonist once-removed . . . I was a step-mother!

The kids and I have enjoyed a good relationship, and sparks that were struck on occasion would have happened if we were blood kin. But in this particular type of exchange . . . (what *was* the subject that night!) . . . Allen had a logical, if disconcerting, tendency to get defensive. If I charged in too hard . . . even to defend his argument . . . he would switch sides suddenly, and it became three against one. I tried to learn when backing off was the better part of valor.

Ah . . . maybe that's why I saved those pages! Because handling an argument in that sensible way was not the norm for me, but rather the exception. Most of the time I jump in, shoot from the hip, and wind up losing the point I am trying to make. Those pages *better* go in "The Box." They could be a collector's item.

Needless to say, all of the above is totally unrelated to a civilized entry in a nightly journal to record the events of the day . . . and is only to be used as a last resort to ward off a potential explosion.

Writing is also said to be great therapy in trying to cope with grief. Again and again, I have heard and read that when the lava dome begins to build up in your chest to the point of being unbearable, it can relieve the pressure if you write down the memories that threaten to overwhelm you. Not to worry if they aren't in any particular order, or if they are good memories, or bad memories, or even whether they are factually correct. You aren't even bound to read back what you have written. It is the simple act of *writing* it that is supposed to bring relief . . . breaking that downward emotional spiral.

To me that makes great sense. I'm sure it should help . . . it's the same ploy as my venting anger by trying to articulate ideas that wind up in "The Drawer."

Yet isn't it strange . . . when it might have helped the most, I couldn't bear to pick up a pencil.

On Anger

Anger tears me up inside . . . My own . . . or anyone else's.

How often I have heard people say, "I really blew my stack! It made me feel so much better!" Though I've never had the guts to ask, I wonder each time if they had any kind of emotional hangover afterward.

I have learned the hard way, that for the momentary satisfaction I may get from a flare-up, there will be a heavy price to pay in the sleepless replays that inevitably follow. Sorry to say, this does not preclude my getting mad . . . I have inherited what my mother used to call her Greek Temper . . . but, with rare, painful exceptions, I usually manage to keep the steam within . . . until I can get away by myself for a primal scream or two . . . At least, by so doing, there are no lethal words left hanging forever in the air.

There is rarely, if ever, a winner in any heated verbal exchange. No one's opinion is altered . . . probably only reinforced . . . and so much more is dredged up than the issue of the moment. Don't be too quick to congratulate yourself on your wondrous restraint, at those times when you stopped short of saying something devastating and held your tongue. Rest assured that, down the line, the first time you really lose it . . . out it will pour.

Other people's anger I find devastating, as well. Strangers screaming anonymously at each other can trigger an anxiety in me that is very hard to shake off. When it is someone known and cared for, it is almost unbearable.

As a child, I can remember hearing my parents quarrel. They used to have some real barn-raisers . . . probably because they were very much in love, not just toler-

ating each other. However, I would be shattered. The
moment either one would become aware of this, the fight
would come to an abrupt stop . . . but I could still feel
the lingering anger there. It was only after they had
kissed and really made up that I could draw a deep
breath again.

Isn't it strange . . . I haven't thought of that in years.

Because anger, in general, is such a personal trauma, I
have tried to find ways around it. Surprisingly, this gets a
little easier with each year that passes. I am finally convinced, at this late date, that smiling and shrugging takes
a lot less out of you than fury. Especially concerning the
little things that don't really matter. It may be momentarily frustrating to your opponent . . . but by the time
the subject comes up again at some later date, your differences may have dissolved completely.

One would assume that this behavior would lead to all
sorts of deep frustrations . . . even total psychological
disaster. I'm sure those who are supposed to know about
these things would be horrified. But remember, all I'm
doing, *for the moment,* is simply turning my back on what
upset me . . . not putting a lid on it. If the anger
doesn't dissipate rapidly, believe me, the volcano will
blow.

I don't consider this being a wimp, but rather someone
interested in the conservation of energy. Also, it saves
the big artillery for a battle that really matters.

There is just one minor detail I haven't quite got
worked out as yet. That is how to instantly make the
distinction between what is trivial, as opposed to what is

worth fighting for . . . all within a second, when your
emotions are just this side of flash point. Aside from that,
the system works swell.

Where I find the smile-and-shrug approach particularly useful is in coping with the myriad of unimportant
irritants that daily threaten to send one over the edge.

Take driving, for example . . . the perfect barometer
by which to gauge how uptight one is without knowing it.
If I am in an especially acute state of hassle . . . with
twice as many things to do than time in which to do them
. . . I make a *conscious* effort to relax completely as I get
behind the wheel. It's almost like fastening an emotional
seat belt. For one thing, it keeps me from carrying the
pressures on to the next stop. More importantly, it
makes driving a helluva lot safer . . . even enjoyable.

When the tension is more than skin-deep, nothing will
make it surface faster than having some idiot in front of
you wait to put his left turn signal on until the light
changes . . . or park and swing his door open to get
out, just as you are passing. It is at times like this that I let
fly with a somewhat creative verbal barrage . . . then
pray no one can lipread. Unfortunately, this fails to serve
as the tension release it should be. *I* wind up feeling
foolish . . . while the joker goes his way, completely
unaware that I even exist.

What finally percolated through this thick skull of
mine is that all this is a tremendous waste of time. If I
don't feel *better* for getting mad, why do it? I now try very
hard to grin and give way. On those occasions when it is
really warranted . . . let's say some cretin runs the yellow as it's turning red . . . I may allow myself the luxury

of a resigned little shake of the head. My rage I save for bigger things.

All of this could sound as if I am the one who is generally put upon, and that I never make a dumb mistake. Which, of course, is true.

On Jealousy

How do you describe jealousy? In what way do you define that ugly emotion? I thought it would be one of the easy ones to pin down, but when I try, it keeps dodging away. That's what makes it so insidious . . . it won't come out in the open . . . it likes dark places.

In the interest of being totally honest, I must say that I have never been jealous of *things*. As far back as I can remember, if someone had something we couldn't afford, which happened a lot, it didn't occur to me to be jealous of the fact. If I was in contention for something and lost out, I would feel bad . . . for myself, because I had wanted to be chosen for whatever it was . . . but that didn't make me *jealous* of whoever won. It wasn't the winner's fault that I wasn't good enough to make it.

Perhaps that's where *envy* fits in the scheme of things. I could, and did, *envy* girls who had lovely hair . . . but that wasn't something to be jealous of . . . they didn't do it on purpose.

Sounds very noble so far, right? Now we get to relationships, which get much more complicated . . . and I
don't come out ahead.

As I remember . . . and I'm the first to admit that
priorities have undergone drastic changes in the interim
. . . in school, it was usually around the fourth or fifth
grades when "best friend"-ships started to form. The
group of friends was still intact, but within the group,
pairs of *closest* friends began to evolve. These were very
important attachments, and you pledged to be inseparable forever . . . or at least through the next semester or
two. Even back then, should my first best buddy, Peggy
Hall, spend too much time with Margaret Miller without
dealing me in too, I began to feel shut out, and a little
sick inside.

Certainly that nasty feeling is left behind in childhood,
as one grows older and wiser. Like hell. About now, *boys*
come into the picture!

As I grew up, and romance became an increasingly
important part of my existence, this same unpleasant
sensation would rear its ugly head from time to time, and
I was forced to recognize the green-eyed monster. Jealousy.

Jealousy hurts just as bad, whether it is warranted or
merely a figment of your own vivid imagination. That's
probably the reason I have never been attracted to the
popular hunk who is driving all the other females crazy.
Even if he should favor me with his attention momentarily, I know there is no way I could deal with all that
competition. This is, no doubt, some form of twisted

insecurity, but knowing what it might be doesn't make it one bit more handleable . . . nor admirable.

Even in situations when I know for a positive fact that there is no cause for jealousy whatsoever . . . I am not proof against it. I have a remarkably clear recollection of a pool party that Allen and I gave, when we were living in Chappaqua, New York. It was a lot of fun, until I began to notice that one of the girls present found my husband terribly attractive. The fact that she was right didn't make me feel any better.

In all fairness, Allen was so busy being a good host, he was more or less an innocent bystander . . . but wherever he was, somehow she was there too . . . laughing inordinately at whatever he said. As per usual, for me, the madder I got inside, the more outgoing and "charming" I became, and Allen knew something was up. It was a little subplot going that none of the guests would ever have suspected. They wouldn't even have noticed the lady's (see how "charming"?) preoccupation because they weren't infected by the jealousy virus. Even Allen didn't know *what* was bugging me, but he knew his girl well enough to know that something was.

The evening was a success, the guests went home happy . . . one, I'm glad to say, not quite as happy as she may have had in mind. Together, Allen and I began straightening up the usual party debris, as we always did, rather than face it next morning. I gradually became aware of the fact that I was flitting around picking stuff up, while Allen was standing quietly in the middle of the floor, just watching . . . waiting for me to wind down. When I did, he took me by the shoulders, and said gently, "Now, are you going to tell me what you're so mad at me about?"

Direct questions like that are really unfair! They require an answer in kind . . . direct, quiet, well-stated . . . and I was in no mood for *that* nonsense. Whatever I might have come up with would have sounded like the petulant, jealous witch that I was feeling at the moment . . . so I did what any red-blooded American wife would do under the circumstances . . . I said, "Nothing!!!" Allen, however, was never lacking in persistence. (Or I wouldn't have married him, wouldn't be standing there feeling foolish . . . *That* almost made me mad all over again.) So, with a few bitchy asides from me, we eventually talked it out.

In the course of the conversation, he pointed out that *I* was, innately, an incorrigible flirt, whether I was aware of it or not, and though he had seen it, he knew it was a sort of reflex action that didn't mean anything. While he didn't like it a lot, he wasn't bothered by it because he was secure in knowing I loved *him*, and he trusted me completely.

Well, try and win an argument with someone unfair enough to use logic against you. Bluster as I might, I knew he was absolutely right. I *was* a flirt . . . though I thought of it as harmless party badinage. Could it be that I had spotted our overly attentive guest earlier, because I recognized the symptoms? I wasn't about to admit such a thing, of course, but I did gain a new perspective from that conversation. For the first time, I realized that Allen actually didn't understand what jealousy felt like . . . it simply wasn't in his lexicon. He was too smart to give it houseroom.

I should have been grateful for that, and I was.
Did I take it as a learning experience? Nope.

With all my heart, I wish they had picked some other
color besides green for such a vicious emotion. Hopefully it is only by coincidence, but green happens to be
my absolute favorite color of all.

In any event, it's too late to do anything about it now.
It would be awkward to say, "I turned puce with jealousy!"

On Guilt

The guilt trip is one we all take in one form or another.
For some, it's more a way of life than a journey.

So many ethnic groups claim guilt as their private pre-
rogative . . . it's almost like a school tie. But perhaps
it's not an accident of birth, so much, as the nature of the
individual beast. I'll match my WASP guilt with any chal-
lengers.

Obviously, we are not talking heavy guilt here . . .
just the ordinary everyday garden variety through which
we wade on a daily basis. Try as we may, some of us still
screw up.

If you don't do something you think you *should* do . . .
you feel guilty.

If you *do* something you think you shouldn't . . . it's even worse.

If you *say* you'll do something and then you don't do it . . . well! . . . you might as well pack it in.

Actually . . . taken in moderation, a little guilt never hurt anybody. Through my growing up years, it certainly helped this child separate right from wrong. Sure, I made *big* mistakes . . . but at least I knew the difference.

My folks used the system of positive reinforcement on me, as a kid . . . the same method that good dog trainers use successfully today. They would praise me for what I did right . . . then, when I did something wrong, they didn't actually punish me, but, oh boy, I knew I had made them unhappy! That hurt more than anything, because I was really anxious to please . . . as my dogs are today. Child psychologists may be turning purple, but it worked. Mom and Dad had me paper-trained in no time!

Squaring up . . . what it did do was set a pattern that has stayed with me all my life. Tell me I'm doing okay and I will break my neck to do better. Tell me I'm rotten, and that is exactly how I will be, no matter how hard I *try*. Admittedly, I don't have a corner on that market . . . it works that way for most on the receiving end. It would be nice if more of those dishing it out were aware of the fact.

Don't misunderstand. My folks corrected and criticized a *lot*, and I was never allowed to "get by" with anything . . . but they laced it all with enough approbation to keep me interested and trying. (Sometimes *very*

trying!) The result was I never had that negative feeling
of "I can't do anything right."

Whether or not it was justified, I can't say, but so many
of my friends seemed to make a hobby of bad-mouthing
their parents. At a given age, I realize, that is par for the
course . . . but some never outgrew it.

In the context of present-day complexities and problems and fragmented family life, or lack thereof . . .
parent/child relationships of fifty years ago don't seem
very pertinent. But buried in there somewhere is a core
of love and mutual respect that *could* be of value even
today.

Probably having something to do with being an only
offspring, I don't think I ever let off steam about my
parents to anyone on the outside. When I was mad at my
folks, I didn't take out an ad in the school paper. I either
blew up at *them*, and we talked it out, or it all sorted itself
out and went away. Somewhere along the way I skipped
"rebel." It never occurred to me to disagree with my
parents just *because* they said something . . . only if I
disagreed with *what* they said.

I am not saying this is good or bad . . . it's simply the
way it was.

My mother clued me in very early on the fact that no
matter how many people you think you can fool . . . or
lie to . . . the only one on this earth who won't hold still
for it is the individual looking back at you in the mirror.

You know me well enough by now to know that, with
my hyper imagination, it didn't take long before that
mirror image became another person to me . . . one
who could bring me up short, and force me to stop and
think. More than once in my life, I have found myself

trying to avoid the eyes in that reflection . . . and I
realized I was in big trouble. Take it from me, it is not
easy to comb your hair, or put on your makeup under
these circumstances. That other person simply will not
go away. You know that, sooner or later, the two of you
are going to have to address what is on your mind.

The system still works. Not so dumb, that mother of
mine.

The same reflection can be effective in keeping your
feet on the ground when the *good* things happen, as well.
If something especially gratifying comes along, or you
did something that turned out better than you had
hoped, it's an easy temptation to get a little carried away
with yourself, momentarily. Well, leave it to that damned
mirror image to bring you right down to size. I can *hear* it
saying, "When you start thinking you can walk on water,
honey . . . remember, you can't swim!"

With such a watchdog living in every mirror, you'd
think that would handle the guilt department, right? Forget it.

Outside of a couple of parking violations, my driving
record is pretty clean. Why, then, when I see a police car,
or motorcycle officer, is my instant reaction "What am I
doing wrong!" Talk about your guilt complex.

One day, recently, a black and white pulled up next to
me, and the cop waved. I immediately pulled over. He
followed me, and stopped alongside just long enough to
say, "Hi, Betty! We love your show! Have a nice day!"
. . . and off he went. He almost made an arrest, all right
. . . cardiac.

Do you get many letters asking for donations to various causes? Unless you live on Mount Rushmore, it's a safe bet that you do.

Charity mail requests have multiplied by geometric progression. It has become a separate business of its own, with companies of professionals designing those pleas for many major charities . . . directly reminding us of our relative good fortune compared to someone else's need. There is certainly nothing wrong with this. We often need reminding . . . there are simply so *many* genuine and worthy causes asking for the same charity dollar that competition becomes intense. Each day's mail contains a wide choice of these. The ones that stir our conscience . . . or our subconscious guilt . . . the most are the ones to which we respond. "Genuine" and "worthy" are key words here . . . if you have any doubt, investigate first, by all means.

The number of these requests continues to burgeon to the point that they run the risk of canceling each other out. Because we can't give to them all, tiny calluses begin to form on the very conscience they are trying to reach . . . and it becomes easier not to respond to any. That would be too bad.

So how do we handle it? Throwing them at the ceiling and picking the one that sticks is neither a reliable nor generous way of choosing. Pick those relating to your particular interests, check them out, then give what you can. No gift is too small . . . think how much could be accomplished if *everybody* gave *something* to *somebody*. Let your conscience be your guide.

See? I told you so! Guilt isn't *all* bad.

On Sex

Can you remember watching television before sex went public?

What did talk shows *talk* about before they discovered surrogate sex, and orgasms for fun and profit?

We know by now, do we not, that I have a strong tendency to oversimplify? So just chalk this off as a random observation . . . but, judging by the amount of diverse sex information that assails us on any given day . . . we must be learning a *lot*. More than some of us even thought we needed to know. We certainly can't plead innocence anymore as an excuse for digression . . . if we don't know the hows, whys, and why nots by now, we just haven't been listening.

Let's play "whatif" for a minute.

Suppose someone had been shipwrecked on a desert island for about twenty-five years, and was just rescued last week. Wouldn't you love to watch his face the first time he flips on his TV set in the afternoon? Or goes to what would be considered an average movie today? We've come a long way, baby.

Poor old privacy has taken a real beating . . . since some of the most intimate moments have taken center stage. Having never been a voyeur, that really doesn't turn me on . . . quite the reverse, if you must know. Sex is so great unto itself . . . but as a spectator sport, it leaves something to be desired . . . to coin a phrase. Obviously, this is the minority viewpoint.

It is also probably somewhat generational.

Don't forget . . . I grew up during the period when what we now think of as film classics . . . were *new* movies!

I can remember getting carried away watching a warm love scene culminate in a tender kiss . . . as the kiss built in passionate intensity, the music would swell to a crescendo . . . and the camera would pan up to the wind-tossed trees outside the window. If we were very lucky, we might get waves crashing on a beach . . . before the fade to black, when our imagination took over.

Today, of course, the camera hangs in there until we get right down to the nitty-gritty . . . sometimes more gritty than nitty.

Salome knew what she was doing . . . gradually removing those seven veils so provocatively. If she had started without them, she might have been just another chunky lady.

And speaking of titillation . . . I often wonder how the poor stripper makes a living these days . . . now that nudity is almost commonplace? Does her audience holler, "Put it on!"? An ecdysiast could well be an endangered species. Not true, really . . . the gender has changed, that's all. Now, it's the boys who are bumping and grinding their way into the hearts of America . . . in nightclubs for women . . . all across the country.

While I am getting this off my chest . . . sorry, there is no *way* you can discuss this subject . . . I might as well try and figure out what I am talking about. (Why should I start now?)

We were discussing old movie love scenes, before I digressed . . . where they didn't have to bed down on camera to project passion. Just a look across a crowded room could do the trick. At least it could for me.

The *kiss* is where the talent begins . . . and sometimes ends. Speaking from long research as an enthusiastic participant . . . the first kiss should leave some room for improvement. The format, these days, is often . . . boy meets girl, boy likes girl, girl digs boy . . . and they start immediately chewing each other's makeup off . . . *then* they find out each other's names.

That technique may be all right as a learning experience for kids, but once the training wheels are off, a little finesse leaves somewhere to go. We know where that is, but why rush it? . . . getting there is half the fun. Both on and off the screen.

If he tries to give me his best shot on that first kiss, I lose interest fast. Being a pigeon for romance, however . . . let someone give me the sweet tender-but-strong approach, and he has my attention. Tender, not wimpy . . . strong, not macho . . . it's the subtly blended package that works on me every time. But why am I telling you all this . . . unless, of course, you are taking notes? Actually, what we do on our own time is our own business.

Television, today, has loosened up quite a bit, wouldn't you say? Some of the salty dialogue on "The

Golden Girls" may even raise *our* four sets of eyebrows at
the Monday morning script reading. There are network
people from the Compliance and Practices Department,
who are the watchdogs for that sort of thing . . . and
sometimes their leniency is surprising. We even make a
bet among ourselves, now and then, as to whether a line
will make it to Friday night taping . . . and once in a
great while, one or another of us will ask that a line be
changed, if it doesn't sit well with whoever has to say it.

I can't recall any specific problems in that regard on
"The Mary Tyler Moore Show" . . . although, I was not
around on a day-to-day basis. Even rotten Sue Ann Nivens, with all her claims of sexual action (I never believed
her for a minute) . . . was so ridiculous, she was never
taken seriously enough for objection.

Blanche Devereaux, our Golden Girls swinger, says
things that are absolutely outrageous . . . she makes
poor old Sue Ann look like a virgin . . . but only *rarely*
does anyone take exception. Rue says that once or twice
she *has* received a call from her Daddy in Oklahoma,
saying, "Honey . . . you tell those writers to lighten up
on you . . . they are gettin' a little clo-o-se to the
li-i-ne!"

When I used to appear with some regularity on the
Jack Paar "Tonight Show," we had to be careful to keep
our mental editors in good working order . . . not always easy when you like each other and are having fun.

I remember one night, talking about the way people
would come to me when they were looking for a dog
. . . (never mind!) . . . because they knew I was always
trying to place unwanted puppies. I said it made me feel

like a *procuror*. Well, mercy, Miss Scarlett, the Programs
and Practices folk went into an instant huddle to see if
that would have to be bleeped for the West Coast. (The
show was done live in New York, and delayed for the
different time zones, so that it would air late.) They decided that, in the context in which it was used, it was
okay. One night, shortly thereafter, Jack made television
history when he walked off the show . . . during a taping, and in front of a live audience. He was absolutely
furious that because he had used the term "water closet"
in telling a joke, they were going to bleep it as unaccept-
able. He kept on walking . . . to Hong Kong. It was
several weeks before everybody kissed and made up.

Back in the dark ages . . . 1949 . . . when I first
started in television . . . Faye Emerson was a big star of
her own show, out of New York, and she caused a little
heavy breathing because her necklines were considered
"plunging." Innuendo was subliminal, if at all. On "Father Knows Best," Robert Young and Jane Wyatt were so
pristine, they must have had those children by osmosis.

Al Jarvis and I were doing a talk show in Los Angeles
for five and a half hours a day, six days a week. I was his
girl Friday . . . as well as Monday through Saturday.
Along with guests and songs and special features, we
managed to squeeze in an average of fifty commercials a
day . . . our record was fifty-eight . . . with not a sani-
tary napkin or a douche among them. Somehow, we
managed to find plenty of other things to sell.

Spending that many hours a day on camera, un-
scripted, you did a lot of talking . . . but minding your
mouth wasn't as difficult then as it has become. There

were invisible built-in guidelines, beyond which was automatically off-limits. Today, it's a little like walking across a swamp on a footbridge . . . one misstep, and you are in the muck. But one man's muck is another man's humor . . . and it is all a very subjective game. You can only try to set your own standards of taste, and hope for the best.

For better or worse, art reflects life . . . it does not set an example in order to improve the audience. It was ever thus . . . we didn't just invent that. In television shows of late, there has been a concerted effort to play down scenes depicting excessive casual drinking, and to minimize dope-related humor. Among other things, this has been brought about through public pressure . . . in direct proportion to the efforts made to improve the situation in real life.

Since the AIDS epidemic has attained such a high profile . . . and made promiscuity a more dangerous game . . . it will be interesting to see how long it will take for the public attitudes to have an effect on screen love scenes. Art reflecting life.

Until that time, we will no doubt continue to see condoms in comic strips and TV commercials. That little development happened since Tess left . . . two years ago. What would she think? She would be sad that we had reached such a point. What would she say? She would keep a straight face and say something like, "I had a beautiful condom . . . on the sixth floor in Century Towers."

If the situation should get so acute that sex is no longer *in* . . . Blanche may have to resort to arts and crafts.

On Enthusiasm

What do you generally notice first about someone?

With me, it's hands. Long before I can tell you the color of a man's eyes, I will have seen his hands. If they are neither too rough nor too limp . . . if they look capable and strong, yet gentle . . . I will check the rest of him out immediately.

Watching someone handle a child or an animal is particularly revealing. The person can be giving you all the lip service in the world about how much he or she *loves* children, or animals . . . yet the hands remain stiff and impersonal. Believe me, whatever little creature is being handled responds accordingly.

Hands may be what I *see* first . . . what keeps me hanging around is a quality difficult to define . . . genuine enthusiasm. Strange as it seems, it is not all that prevalent.

There is such a subtle but vital distinction between gushing and honest enthusiasm that, unfortunately, one can often be mistaken for the other. Even worse . . . you can find yourself slipping over that fine line, until "genuine enthusiasm" quickly turns into carrying on, ad nauseum. Nothing is easy.

As a sweeping generalization, however, for my money enthusiasm is a virtue, no matter one's age or gender. You can't be that way about everything, certainly . . . but heaven help you if you aren't that way about *something!* There is no bigger turnoff to me than the Kool Kat who is so laid-back, he refuses to be surprised or excited or thrilled about *anything.* He doesn't commit himself on any subject to the point that he can't pull back, so he often gives the impression of being right. I wonder if he ever really falls in love?

No . . . I'll take someone who may be wrong sometimes . . . but, boy, he's wrong with enthusiasm. He falls in love the same way.

Allen Ludden could just possibly have been the one who invented enthusiasm. If he liked something, he liked it a *lot.* If he didn't, he made it abundantly, if indiplomatically, clear. There were occasions when things might have been a little simpler with a tad *less* enthusiasm. But nothing to Allen was ever ho-hum, and it made life more interesting for those around him.

Allen's garden was his hobby and his joy. Every Christmas he would plant hanging baskets for close friends . . . whether they had anyplace to hang them or not. Also, his fervor for cutting things back was equaled only by that of our gardener, Mr. Sakamoto . . . I would shudder when I'd see the two of them pick up pruners and shears. Now and then I would get downright hostile . . . but when things soon leafed out lovelier than ever, I had to admit the zeal had paid off.

Allen's love for the garden continued to grow . . . he was enrolled in a landscape architecture course at Pierce College, which he didn't live to complete.

Someone else who has a corner on the enthusiasm market is Mel Tormé. Mel and his wife Ali are close friends, and I see them quite often . . . and I have yet to find something that *doesn't* interest Mel. He is knowledgeable on a wide variety of subjects . . . aside from his genius in the music field. He reads *everything* . . . devours movies of any era, has a number of collections, regarding which he is passionate. Offhand, I don't ever remember hearing Mel give a lukewarm assessment of anything . . . it's either the best . . . or the worst. Even when he thinks it's the worst, he does it with great verve.

I'm sure I am overstating the case, but in any event his approach is a lot more fun than indifference . . . and whether you agree with him or not, he stimulates a response. That same intensity is what sets Mel's awesome talent above the rest in his field. Bland, he ain't.

One is only as big as the world he is interested in. I don't know who said that, but I wish I had. We use such a small part of what we are capable of . . . often because we let ourselves slip into a chronic "Who cares?" attitude. We devote a tremendous amount of energy these days to physical exercise . . . or at least *talking* about it . . . let's not sell *mental* exercise short.

End of speech.

"Genuine enthusiasm" and "a positive attitude" must be at least first cousins. Would you say that, for the most part, you have a positive attitude?

Careful how you answer.

Say yes, and you can easily find yourself sneered at, patronized, condescended to, dubbed "little Pollyanna" . . . and, in toto, shot down. It happens.

There seems to be a rather large portion of the population who get their jollies by pointing up every negative they can find. For them the rule is apparently reversed . . . guilty until proven innocent. I'm not talking about the people who make their living as professional critics . . . I mean the everyday, allegedly normal people we all know, who give life in general a bad review. These folk revel in being wretched. If they ever found themselves liking anything at first blush, I'm sure they'd be miserable.

A recurring question that usually turns up somewhere in an interview is "How do you always manage to be so . . . up?" I get the distinct impression they have stopped just short of adding "How phony can you get?"

Phony? Not at all. It is self-preservation. Cliché or not, accenting the positive beats the hell out of the constant negative . . . especially if *you* are the only one you live with.

It often strikes me that I am probably at my most obnoxious when I'm feeling low inside. I overcompensate, make bad jokes, have too much to say, and undoubtedly drive everyone to the point of doing me bodily harm. I say it strikes me, but not hard enough . . . For the life of me, I can't keep my mouth shut.

Oh, the negatives are all there, and I won't deny that sometimes it feels so good to let 'em rip and get it out of your system. But you'd better have a round-trip ticket in your hot little fist to get back to at least neutral ground, or you can wind up in Depression City.

My sixth grade teacher said something once that really stuck. (Who says I don't have a memory . . . that *had* to be in the dark ages!) Her name was Mrs. Thoroughgood, which should have been enough right there. She got very angry in class one day . . . her eyes filled up, and she said, "I only cry when I'm hurt, and when I'm mad. And I *never* cry unless I know I can stop!" Sure enough, not a tear fell. More times I've wondered how she managed that.

A friend tells the story of a janitor in his building who would sing up a storm sometimes while he was working. One day my friend said, "Willie, you sure sound happy."

"No," said Willie. "I'm trying to *get* happy."

Willie sings. I make bad jokes.

But we do it with enthusiasm.

V

HEART OF
THE MATTER

On Memory

Any momentary lapse in recall is immediately blamed on advancing age. And for the most part with good reason. However, my memory has *always* been lousy. I could memorize a script in five minutes, but drew a blank as to where I had dinner last Tuesday . . . and with whom. And this was in high school. It probably happened even before that, but I can't remember.

That's why, whenever I have been asked to write my "memoirs," or someone wants to collaborate on the story of my life, I pass. There is just no way I can fill in the blanks, some of which are not all that trivial . . . a first marriage, a whole television *series*, ("A Date with the Angels"). It's as though these things happened to somebody else, and I was out of the country at the time.

I'm not being coy. It's scary. Other things that occurred before, after, or during are Lucite clear . . . but chronology has never been my best thing. If it weren't for a raft of old interviews, I wouldn't know half the places I've been.

That's why the people who keep journals are so smart. Carol Burnett told me she never goes to sleep at night without writing *something* of the day . . . whether a little or a lot. She not only has a record of what happened, but even how she felt about it at the time.

How I wish I had been smart enough to do that. I was even off to a good start . . . and then blew it.

Remember those fat little five-year diary books? . . . They are no doubt still around. They were about 4×5 . . . leather- or plastic-bound . . . and they had a lock with a tiny key. For every day there would be space for five years on a single page . . . considering the size of the book, you couldn't go into a great amount of detail on your life. Well . . . I kept one of those things faithfully . . . for seven years. That's a diary book and two-fifths! . . . (you could have figured that out, I guess) . . . complete, without skipping a day. If, for any reason, I did neglect it for a night or two, I would go back and catch up.

The years covered were from the age of almost ten to almost seventeen . . . unfortunately, not the most dynamic period of my life. Also, my priorities were strange . . . frequently, I would report what we had for dinner. (Keep in mind the space I had to work with.) There were several pressed leaves and flowers . . . carefully saved, but not explained. I did, however, record at some length a terrible crush on Fred Astaire . . . *and* Ginger Rogers.

Then . . . I went from crush to a deep, serious, and abiding love . . . for Nelson Eddy. I wasn't jealous of Jeanette MacDonald . . . I *was* Jeanette MacDonald! I saw *Naughty Marietta* thirty-two times on its first time around, *Rose Marie* twenty-nine times, and *Maytime* twenty-six . . . not including the countless times afterward, through the years. The monetary investment wasn't quite as monumental as it may sound . . . in those days, admission was forty cents tops . . . often less. I now have all three of those films on cassette, and it's nobody's business what the dogs and I watch when no one's around.

Those three pictures were the apex for the MacDonald-Eddy team, as far as I was concerned. After that it became the law of diminishing returns . . . either their subsequent films had diminished in quality, or I had increased in age. But it was only the films that lost some of their luster for me . . . not the stars themselves. I went to every one of their concerts, and I cut their pictures out of magazines until I had boxloads. In all truth, the reason I am in the entertainment business today is due, for the most part, to my feeling for them.

Years later, I followed Jeanette in summer stock in Warren, Ohio. She was closing her run in *Bittersweet* one night, and I was opening in *The King and I* the following night. I attended her performance, and was introduced to her backstage. She could not have been warmer or more gracious . . . and you can't imagine the thrill it was to receive a beautiful bouquet in my dressing room the next evening . . . TO BETTY, LOVE, JEANETTE MAC-DONALD!

Later, back in California, our paths crossed again on several occasions, and she always treated me like a dear friend. The Jeanette MacDonald Fan Club is not only still in existence, but it is an enormous international organization. Each year, they have a beautiful formal banquet in her honor hosted by her husband, Gene Raymond . . . they are presently celebrating their fiftieth year!

I never met Nelson Eddy. I saw him once . . . from a distance . . . in the hall at NBC, but I lacked the intestinal fortitude to approach him. I've always regretted that.

But I digress! And now I can't remember what we were talking about. Oh, yes . . . memory.

Anyway, after seven years of faithful diary-keeping, just when it was beginning to get interesting . . . I up and quit!

Figuring it is never too late to make up for lost time, I thought to benefit by Carol Burnett's example, and bought a pretty little bedside notebook with pencil attached. I forget to write in it.

So my chronology is all screwed up, and *so* some chunks of my life are AWOL . . . I'm just grateful for those things that have remained so sharply etched. That's what makes this book such a delightful adventure for me . . . it's a chance to rummage around in my head and come up with all sorts of things I had no idea were there.

How erratically my alleged mind works, or doesn't, is only my problem, and I don't spend a lot of time fretting about it, since it won't affect anyone else. But then I get to thinking . . . and this is usually pretty late into the night . . . in the beginning, all history was predicated on the memories of the older members of the society. It was either handed down, word-of-mouth, or scrawled on the rock of the cave. Do we really want to take the word of somebody who writes on the walls? And who among us hasn't played the game of telling one person a story, who repeats it to someone, who, in turn, tells it to the next person, and so on. By about the fourth repetition, the original story is unrecognizable. Multiply that by a few centuries. *All history!*

Before I get too frightened, I generally fall asleep.

Admittedly, even the scientific community doesn't understand the mechanics or the hardware of memory. One psychobiologist, Gary Lynch, of the University of California, Irvine, called it "the black hole at the center of neurobiology." With the interest in the subject, and the research that is going on, more and more is being discovered. It is fascinating. A state-of-the-art computer can store bits of information numbering in the billions. The human mind, it is estimated, can store *100 trillion bits!*

Each of us is walking around with the equivalent of a largely unexplored planet on our shoulders . . . and we are using only a fraction of it. If a way is ever found to unlock those stored bits of information, there is no limit to what we will discover . . . about ourselves, as well as about the world around us.

All history!!?!

On Memories

Memories are only distantly related to memory itself . . . another branch of the family entirely. Memories should sometimes carry a warning label . . . EXPLOSIVE MATERIAL.

With the possible exception of amnesiacs and congen-
ital idiots, everyone has a collection of memories of some
kind. They can be among our most cherished posses-
sions. The problem with the damned things is . . . they
are completely unmanageable. Both the glorious ones
and the excruciating ones are woven together so tightly,
it is virtually impossible to call up one without exhuming
the other.

If you aren't careful, memories can get the bit in their
teeth and run with you . . . taking you over the jumps,
whether you like it or not, only to dump you unceremoni-
ously . . . leaving that hollow ache that has to wear itself out.

For instance . . . every now and then, around twilight time, I could swear I hear the front door open, and
then the familiar "Darlin'?" It was Allen's Texas version
of the old "Honey, I'm home!" . . . This is after six
years.

Sure, it hurts. But think how much more it would hurt
if I didn't *have* the memories . . . that kind of void
would really be tough to handle. No, I'll settle for it . . .
I hope I'll always hear it. "Darlin'?"

Music is the most evocative . . . it can really play
tricks on you. The song "Memory" from the Broadway
musical *Cats* was written with me in mind . . . of this I
was certain, until I discovered how many others feel exactly the same way. Wherever there is background music,
it's a safe bet that sooner or later they will get to "Memory." One should be used to it by now. Well, no matter
how far away or unobtrusive the music may be . . . the
first two notes of that melody will cut through *whatever*

else is going on. Hopefully, no one else is aware of this, and we don't miss a beat. But privately I have a very warm feeling inside . . . a hurt *good*.

In the computer we call our brain, what department is in charge of memory selection? Because they do a pretty sloppy job. They let whole blocks of major events in your life blur around the edges . . . yet *trivia* will be carved in stone. There are some fascinating studies in progress on this very subject . . . and, as more is learned, that whole memory department will have to get on the ball . . . or heads will roll.

Memories aren't all sad-making by a long shot . . . we'd be in big trouble if they were. Some make you laugh.

In the exact same location on Sunset Boulevard, I had two separate dog encounters that occurred years apart . . . but within an *eighth* of a block of each other.

The first happened quite a few years ago, during my "tropical fish period" . . . when I got completely caught up in that fascinating hobby.

My mother was with me, and we were driving home from yet another trip to Aquarium Stock . . . I think it was neon tetras that I had to replace this time. To transport these little beauties, they are put in a plastic bag full of water, which is then tied at the top. It keeps a container from sloshing around, and is less traumatic for the fish. Mom was to hold this carefully aloft, all the way home.

Suddenly . . . just past the Bel Air Gate on Sunset, in heavy late-afternoon traffic . . . I see this beautiful little pug dog, dodging in and out of traffic, completely bewildered. I pulled over under a NO STOPPING AT ANY TIME sign, got out . . . and not wanting to scare him even more . . . knelt down and called to him. Bless his heart, he came running as if I was his oldest friend, and I put him in the car. *Now* my mother has to steady a frightened strange dog with one hand, while she is still juggling a bag of fish in the other. We made it safely home, oddly enough, and by morning we were able to trace his worried owners, by calling all the veterinarians in the area. He went home, to tell everybody he'd slept with Betty White.

One night, years later, it was about eleven P.M., and I was driving home alone after a taping of "Mama's Family" . . . I was still in makeup and eyelashes, with my hair piled on top of my head, as Ellen always wore it on the show.

I got to the exact same spot on Sunset, and had to jam on my brakes to avoid several cars stopped in odd positions across the road. Running in and out of the headlights were two enormous fawn Great Danes. I pulled under my favorite NO STOPPING sign . . . talk about déjà vu . . . and got out without even thinking of what I would do. It took some coaxing and the help of a sympathetic young man, but we finally got both of them . . . a male and a female . . . into the backseat of my car.

Everyone was so relieved, and before I could explain, they all drove off . . . happy in the knowledge that this strange-looking lady had retrieved her dogs. So I'm sitting there on an empty street, and I have two Great Danes in my car that I can't take home with me because of my own dogs.

On a chance, I drove back to the Bel Air Neighborhood Patrol station at the Bel Air Gate. I walked in, with
all my makeup and my upswept hair . . . looking like a
hooker who'd lost her way . . . and said, "Excuse me, I
have a pair of Great Danes!"

Well, it took a few minutes to sort it all out, but those
nice people knew the dogs . . . who, incidentally were
behaving like angels all this time . . . knew where they
escaped from . . . and would take them back home. I'd
lucked out again.

Never do I pass that spot . . . which I do every single
day while going to and from work . . . without smiling.
I keep my eyes on the road in front of me, however . . .
I'm afraid to look around for fear of what I might find
this time.

Some memories are even well-behaved enough to
come when they are called. Once in a while, if I have
trouble getting to sleep at night, I try to set my mind to
something I've enjoyed, and relive it. It's like turning
pages in an album . . . or playing back a videocassette.
I have a whole set of these . . . and I must say, the
quality is terrific.

The ones I play back most often are two trips Allen and
I made to Ireland.

We were the guests of Mrs. Kingman Douglass . . .
formerly Adele Astaire, Fred's sister and brilliant dancing partner on Broadway. . . . Dellie had actually been
the star of the act. She was the toast of the town, until she
met Lord Cavendish, and retired from her dancing career to become his Lady.

Following his death, she remarried . . . but was widowed, once again. After that, Adele would spend four months every summer at Lismore Castle in southern Ireland . . . which had been her home when she was married to Lord Cavendish.

Fred Astaire's daughter Ava and her husband, Richard McKenzie, were Allen's and my good buddies . . . and it was through them that we met Adele, and the mutual love affair began.

She urged us to come visit her in Ireland . . . Ava and Richard did every summer. Allen was taking me on my first trip to Europe that year . . . exciting enough in itself . . . and we decided that, as long as we were on our feet, we would come home by way of Lismore Castle, and meet the McKenzies there.

It may have been one of the best decisions we ever made.

The castle itself dated back to King John . . . and consisted of two hundred rooms. A portion of these had been beautifully maintained as living quarters . . . tapestried walls, exquisite furniture, some of which had been made on the property over a century ago. Each table or desk held three or four bowls of fresh flowers, brought in every morning by the gardeners . . . from the acres of cutting gardens. Years before, as Lady Cavendish, Adele had had some strategic bathrooms added, which fitted in with the rest of the decor so well you'd think they had grown there. This was not a castle newly renovated for tourists . . . this was a private residence. The "property" was eighteen thousand acres, which included the little picture book town of Lismore.

We spent a week there that trip, and it still seems like something I must have only read about somewhere. First

of all, Dellie herself would have been worth the trip if she
lived in a hovel. Her wit and spice were priceless . . . as
were her stories of earlier days, whenever we managed to
trap her into telling them. Ava, Adele, and I represented
three generations, each twenty years apart . . . but it
was as though we were all the exact same age. I'd say
about fourteen.

Allen and Richard said that as they watched they saw
their wives turn into instant Wuthering Heights. I can
promise you, they were every bit as carried away.

There was a large hall, at the end of which was a door
that led to the rest of the castle . . . wing after wing
containing rooms, now empty, but in good condition
. . . nurseries, maid's quarters off of each bedroom,
carved stairways, alcoves . . . secret places.

We would explore for hours. Ava took us to the small
bedroom in the tower where she would stay as a little
girl, when she came to visit her Aunt Dellie. It had a four-
way panoramic view of the surrounding emerald coun-
tryside . . . with a winding river . . . and wild swans.
We left Wuthering Heights, momentarily, and went
straight to Oz.

One morning we came back from a long walk on the
moors . . . (see what I mean?) . . . when a call came
in from Los Angeles. It was Fred Astaire. He spoke to his
sister and his daughter, of course . . . but he said the
real reason he called, was to complain about a clue someone had given on "Password" that he didn't think was
fair! He had just watched the show, which he did every
day, and the fact that we were in Ireland and the show
had been taped several weeks earlier were only minor

details . . . he got the satisfactory answer he wanted
from Allen.

Being summer, it didn't get dark until around eleven-
thirty at night. After dinner, and a game of our warped
version of Scrabble, Dellie usually went to bed . . . and
the four of us would go out for a last twilight walk before
retiring.

Way down at the end of one of the grassy slopes that
led from the castle was a long double row of ancient yew
trees. They were twisted and gnarled . . . authenti-
cated as dating back to 1100 A.D. . . . where long ago
the monks would stroll in meditation.

This was all that these four bemused Americans
needed. It would be close to midnight by the time we
would reach this spot each night . . . and we would
begin to make up stories about what these trees must
have seen through the centuries. One or another of us
would quietly slip behind a tree, then wait for a scary part
in the story, to leap out unexpectedly. It may sound mild
in the light of day, but under the circumstances, trust me,
it was effective.

Allen couldn't figure out why he could never surprise
us, when it worked so well for everyone else. We didn't
tell him that his white shoes practically glowed in the
dark.

Maybe fourteen was too generous an estimate. Ten-
year-olds might be closer to the truth.

When an experience has been that special, it is taking a
long chance to try and repeat it . . . ever. Nonetheless,
when Adele invited us all back for another week the
following summer . . . there was no way we could re-

sist. Not only was the magic still there . . . if anything, it was even better the second time around. Perhaps we really had been enchanted, after all. Rest well, Dellie dear . . . it was you who cast the spell.

Up-front memories are one thing . . . they will meet you on your own ground and fight fair. But then there is the underhanded variety. Rather than confronting you head-on . . . they sneak up behind you when your guard is down. They can cause you to lose track entirely of what someone else is saying. There is no earthly way of explaining them to anyone . . . sometimes not even to yourself. Don't even try.

Anyone who is missing someone . . . for whatever reason . . . will tell you the same. You can handle the big things. What does you in is the horde of tiny memories that circle your head like gnats . . . the ones no one else can see.

Toadstools on the morning lawn.

A cherry in the bottom of a cocktail glass.

And *why* should anyone's eyes fill at the sight of a lizard in the sun!

You had to be there.

On Friendship

A common misnomer is referring to acquaintances as
friends. There is a big difference, and it's a good idea to
take stock every now and then, and redefine that distinction among the people around us. Not as easy as it
sounds. We're apt to discover we have a *lot* of acquaintances. Or we may be surprised to find we have more
friends than we thought.

One problem is that we expect a friend to be all the
things we like wrapped up in one package. Unfortunately, this occurs with the frequency of an albino dino-
saur.

To be sure, we have the same high hopes in a romantic
relationship, but at least here there are other things
working for us as well . . . genes . . . or jeans . . .
whatever. Something that creates enough of a glow to
make two people believe they have so much in common
. . . temporarily anyway, and occasionally, with luck,
permanently. But in the platonic sense . . . whatever
the individual gender . . . it is not necessary to have a
friend for *all* reasons. If doctors can specialize . . . why
not friends? We *know* how difficult it is to locate a general
practitioner who'll make house calls!

Why not a movie friend? You may not want to see
everything that comes along (God knows!), but you don't

want to miss it all either. And even if you disagree on the movie, it makes for something to talk about afterward.

My closest and oldest friend, (scratch "oldest" . . . make that "friend of long standing") not only enjoys movies, he is a foremost authority on them. He's the author of several important books on the films, and teaches classes on the subject at two different colleges. Hey! . . . when I have a friend for the movies, I get the best . . . I don't fool around! (Steady!)

To be serious . . . while I don't share his knowledge, I do share his interest, and he has no idea how much I've learned to appreciate and enjoy films, thanks to him.

How about a friend with whom you can share some deep interest of your own? With me, it's animals. It's wonderful to know someone who makes me feel so secure, that once in a while I can go on a real animal binge . . . meaning (she hastens to explain) that we can talk animals for hours on end yet know we are in no danger of boring each other. We can't quite indulge that much with anyone else.

For "animals," substitute music . . . cooking . . . sports . . . whatever *your* pleasure. You soon find yourself migrating toward people who feel the same.

Another friend may not have any heavy interests, but likes to gussie up a little and go out for a leisurely dinner and good conversation.

Somebody else likes to kick back, cook dinner at home, then maybe play a game of something.

You can be the one to decide what you feel like doing, and there is someone with whom to enjoy it.

Happily, sometimes these specialists cross over into many other areas of your life . . . a nice serendipity.

Many times these friends may enjoy each other . . .
the game player might join up for a movie, or the dinner
conversationalist will take a stab at Trivial Pursuit. Proceed with caution here, however, or it's possible to wind
up with a group sitting around on dead center, out-
politing each other.

"Well, what would you like to see?"

"I don't care, it's up to you."

"Where shall we eat?"

"Anywhere's fine with me . . . but I can't eat Italian
. . . or Chinese . . . or . . ."

Soon you no longer have a movie friend and a dinner
friend and a game-playing friend. You have a homoge-
nized "bunch." Before you know it, somebody begins to
criticize, someone else picks up the ball . . . soon
you're seeing faults you never noticed. And you wonder
whatever happened to all those fun times you used to
enjoy.

All I'm saying is mix with care . . . I am not saying be
too noble to criticize. It is a proven fact that a little
judicious dishing keeps one's skin clear.

It's one thing for me to blither on here about all these
great ideas for managing all your friends and interests. If
you happen to be at a particular low spot as you read this,
the temptation is to throw the book across the room.

If you have already done that, either literally or figuratively . . . please pick it up and read on. Things do have
a way of changing . . . sometimes even for the better,
believe it or not.

Having choices of friends sounds ironic if you are feeling alone . . . or worse, lonely . . . but there *are* ways

to reach out. You may not even be aware that you have
any special interests, but whether you know it or not
. . . there is *something* you really like, *something* you find
intriguing. Why not start from there . . . let's see what
happens.

There is another designation in the friendship department. In everyone's life there will be one or more who
goes beyond friend. There should almost be a special
term for them . . . Superfriend for now.

They can number anywhere from one to a handful
. . . rarely more . . . over the span of a lifetime. Those
individuals who are *always* there for you, and you for
them . . . no questions asked. Whether you saw them
yesterday or five years ago, you pick up the conversation
where you left off, as if in a time warp.

With these Superfriends, you can give your mental
editor a rest and feel secure in saying anything that pops
into your mind. You can share your victories with them,
in minute detail, knowing they celebrate with you . . .
or you can lay your disasters on them and get strength
and understanding in return.

Knowing this writer, you will probably assume that all
my Superfriends have four legs. Not entirely true . . .
some of them are human. And they know who they are.

On Decisions

Making decisions is not my best thing. That's probably
true of most of us, but some people seem to handle it so
much better. They analyze . . . they weigh . . . they
ponder. I am certain they come up with the right choice
every single time. At least one would hope so, considering the time invested. Try as I will, I can't seem to get the
hang of this approach . . . and wind up shooting from
the hip.

So it follows that I'm a rotten shopper. (I like to go to
the market, sure, but that's *buying,* not *shopping!*) In a
department store, my patience runs out long before I've
waded through all the don't wants to find what I'm looking for. Asking for help can compound the complications
because usually we have to settle the question of whether
I am really who they think I am. More often than not, I
retreat empty-handed. A great way to save money? It
would be if it weren't for the stack of catalogs lying in
wait back home.

Catalogs don't ask you to make hard decisions . . .
they show you a pretty picture, take it or leave it. Having
saved so much at the store, you see, I proceed to get a
little carried away! A color choice may hang me up momentarily, but I can usually handle it. I refuse to clutter
my tiny mind with ominous details such as postage and
handling charges.

As a result, ninety percent of everything I wear, head to toe, comes out of one catalog or another. I've had few disasters, and most of the time, what I saw is what I get. Admittedly, this is not the thriftiest way to tackle shopping . . . but by avoiding the stress of going through a store, I've never had to have mental therapy either. Look how much I save right there.

Some decisions are totally academic . . . such as choosing a puppy or a kitten. The choice is immediately taken out of your hands. He picks you.

If someone else will take care of deciding which restaurant we're going to, I have found myself a way to take the challenge out of the menu after we get there. If I like what I've ordered the first time, then that's what I order every time I go back to that restaurant. Different places, different orders, so it doesn't get monotonous. It does inhibit some of the waiter's creativity, perhaps, but I'm always polite enough to wait through his spiel about the specials. Of course, if it is a restaurant I've never been to before, I'm back in the soup . . . so to speak.

Bea Arthur is a food maven . . . discriminating, knowledgeable, and appreciative . . . and a bit intolerant of someone else's lack in this department. We lunch together every day when we're working, and my unimaginative predictability drives her bananas. We have two regular places we go in the lunchtime allotted, and she knows if we go to the Assistance League dining room I will have the tuna sandwich . . . if it's Columbia Bar and Grill, she can make book that I will opt for the hamburger and french fries . . . neither choice being what could be termed a breakthrough. Bea, meanwhile, is poring over a menu that she must have long since committed to memory, since we have been going to these same two places for months . . . but, somehow, when she orders she makes it sound like an adventure!

Would that all decisions were as readily handled. There are the tough calls . . . the life choices.

In retrospect, the one I agonized over the most should have been the simplest. Allen Ludden proposed to me for a year before I had the good sense to say yes. I must not think about that year I wasted in soul searching.

But there was a lot to consider. I had been happily single for more than ten years. California was my home . . . I commuted to New York to work, because I didn't want to live back there. Marrying Allen would mean pulling up *deep* roots and moving east to stay. No more round-trip ticket in my hot little fist. (I had no way of knowing then, that six years later his job would make it necessary to move back out to the West Coast, where Allen became an instant California convert.)

There were also three children to stir into the equation. Allen's son David, fourteen, Martha, just turned thirteen, and Sarah, ten, were my great and good buddies. While I had watched Allen Ludden on "G.E. College Bowl," and met him on "Password," it was not until we were booked to do a summer play together on Cape Cod that I got acquainted with him . . . and his family.

Together with two chocolate poodle puppies, Willie and Emma, the kids courted me right along with their father, and I fell in love with the whole gang. But the idea of going from pal to stepmother was very scary.

What finally tipped the scale was a matter of priorities.

Simple as that. I faced up to the possibility of never seeing Allen again . . . of continuing my well-adjusted single life . . . which by now, of course, he had warped out of shape altogether. I pictured what it would be like to turn on the television set, through the years, and see this man, again and again . . . realizing I had thrown something away that often doesn't come by even once in a lifetime.

Suddenly the pieces all tumbled into place . . . the obvious answer was finally the only answer. And high time!

Yes!

On Weddings

By now you have gathered that Allen and I had a better than good marriage . . . however it got off to a start that was more like a two-reel comedy.

In talking about decisions earlier, I told you that I wasted a whole year saying no each time Allen proposed. Well, he was not only proposing, he was selling the whole institution of marriage. His previous marriage of eighteen years to Margaret was a wonderful one, until her death from cancer cut it all too short . . . so he knew what he was selling.

It got so that instead of saying hello, he would say,

"Will you marry me?" Sometimes I'd laugh, sometimes I'd get mad . . . but I'd *always* say no.

To show how sure Allen was that persistence would carry the day, he bought a gorgeous gold and diamond wedding ring, and presented it one evening, saying, "This is yours, you know. Someday you'll wear it." "No, I won't!" said she . . . and that was probably one of the nights I got mad. By now, to be sure, I was running scared.

What did he do? For three months he wore that damned ring on a chain around his neck, so I couldn't miss it. It got full of soap, and suntan oil, but he vowed he would only take it off for one reason. Afterward, of course, he told everybody he just hated it when we got married . . . he had to part with the ring!

Because Allen had used up his time off from "Password" to come courting in California . . . when I finally said yes, all they could give him was a long weekend before he had to be back on the show.

At that time, in most states, there was a mandatory blood test and three-day waiting period before getting married . . . except in Nevada. So, in order to have any honeymoon at all, we decided to fly to Las Vegas for the wedding. Are you ready for Mr. Clean and the Girl Next Door getting married in Vegas?

Here was the game plan. Allen was to fly out on a Thursday in June, then on Friday, my mom and dad, Allen, and I would fly to Las Vegas have a celebration dinner, see a show or two . . . and on Saturday morning we'd have the wedding ceremony. The newlyweds would then board a plane to honeymoon for a couple of

days in Laguna Beach, while the bride's parents took
another plane back to Los Angeles. So far, so good.

Come the all-important Thursday, however, Allen was
caught in a gigantic traffic jam in New York, on his way to
Kennedy (then Idylwild) Airport, and missed the only
plane he ever failed to catch in his entire life. When he
got to the airport, he still had a slim chance . . . he
jumped out of the cab, raced in, the man checked his
luggage through in record time . . . then proceeded to
send Allen to the wrong gate!

By that time it was all academic. Practically in tears, he
screamed, "My wedding suit is on the way to California,
and I'm not!" He always remembered a nice lady standing near, who patted his shoulder, saying, "There, there,
Mr. Ludden."

Meanwhile back at the bride's house . . . she was doing battle with not just jitters, but sheer panic. So when
the call came from Allen saying he'd be on a later plane,
she was so warm and understanding . . . through
clenched teeth, she said, "Why don't you just stay
there!" That's the way to comfort a fella, right?

While she didn't deserve it, he was on the next plane,
and by that evening, the lovers *and* the luggage were
reunited, and all was well again. Until the next day, after
we all checked into the Sands Hotel in Las Vegas.

The hotel people, old hands at the game, still fussed
over us as though we were the only wedding party they
had ever met. They put the four of us in a little jitney and
drove us over to a tower building about a quarter of a
mile away. My folks were shown to a lovely double room,
across the hall from an enormous "wedding suite" . . .
complete with a walk-through shower connecting sepa-

rate his and her bathrooms, one in pink, the other all black. Since the wedding was not until the next morning, this was to be my room, and Allen was given a little single room way down the hall!

As we all stood there deciding how long we would take to dress for dinner, Allen suddenly turned ashen . . . "My God! I left my briefcase!" With that, he bolted from the room, and raced on foot all the way back to the main hotel where we had checked in.

When he finally returned, he reported, somewhat breathlessly, that he had found the briefcase still sitting by itself on the floor where he had left it when we were all swept away to our rooms. His trauma was because *in* the briefcase were his wedding presents . . . a lovely jade bracelet for my mother, engraved with THANK YOU, DOLL!, gold cuff links for my father . . . and a beautiful gold and diamond bracelet for his bride, to match the famous wedding ring! Where was that ring? Still safely around his neck? No . . . he had had the jeweler clean it all up, so it, too, was in the briefcase. All this made missing the plane the day before seem like a piece of cake.

After such a stroke of good luck, we four went on to spend a happy, giddy, sentimental evening. The hotel people would no doubt have been amazed if they knew that Allen really did stay in his little room that night . . . and I rattled around the wedding-or-whatever suite, alone.

Early next morning, we went to get our marriage license. Allen took a bellhop along . . . not so much to show us where to go, he claimed, but to help keep me from jumping ship.

The ceremony took place in the wedding suite . . .

(in the living room, not the shower) . . . and the hotel had set up an adjacent room for our "reception" . . . on them! There was a table, at least a block long, filled with enough beautiful canapés to feed a family of twelve for a month, plus champagne bottles by the dozen.

Now, our entire wedding party consisted of my mother and father, the judge who married us, the bellhop, a couple of hotel photographers, and the bride and groom. The photographers split immediately to plant their pictures in the paper, the judge was on his way to another ceremony, the bellhop was on duty, and my dad didn't drink. Mom and Allen and I took one quick glass of champagne, but there were planes to catch. We thought.

It developed that the new summer schedule had gone into effect, and our flight to Laguna had been deleted from that schedule just the week before . . . so sorry. So we *all* piled into the plane back to L.A. My folks kept trying to pretend they didn't know us . . . lest the world think that they were going along on the honeymoon.

After we landed and said our fond good-byes, Allen rented a car and we drove to Laguna. Not having sampled any of the goodies at the Sands (I hope somebody got to really enjoy that spread!) . . . by now we were starving, so we pulled in to a Denny's for a quick sandwich before we got to Laguna. As we walked up to the front door, we could see that the whole group of newsstands carried our picture plastered all over the front pages of the local papers. Someone inside spotted us, stood up in the window, and applauded. We kept right on walking . . . back to the car and Laguna!

What Allen didn't tell me until months later was that,

even in small amounts, champagne always gave him a blinding headache. During those first few weeks, people were so sweet . . . wherever we would go out for dinner, someone was sure to send a bottle of champagne to our table, watch the waiter pour, lift their glasses in a toast, and wait . . . and *wait* . . . for us to join them. We couldn't be rude . . . we certainly couldn't explain across a room . . . we would sip. This no doubt sounds like a golden worry, but my poor darling went through our first two months of wedded bliss with a perpetual secret headache . . . besides the one he married.

The other two members of our wedding adventure, Tess and Horace White, were undaunted by any minor glitches in the overall plan. Their own wedding, forty-two years prior, hadn't won any prizes.

Their two sets of parents were less than thrilled at the idea of them getting married, as both were major bread-winners in their respective families. Reluctant approval was finally obtained, calling for a wedding much later in the year.

Horace had a better idea.

On February 17, accompanied by another couple, they all left work and . . . in the pouring rain . . . proceeded to a justice of the peace and were married. The foursome celebrated over a Chinese dinner, then, at eleven o'clock, Horace took his bride back to her house, kissed her goodnight, and left her, promising to keep their marriage a secret for a while. In this case, *she* was the one who put her wedding ring on a chain and dropped it down her neck out of sight . . . where she could swear it kept growing like Pinocchio's nose.

This went on for two weeks, until the desperate bridegroom chickened out and told his folks . . . without warning Tess. *His* mother called *her* mother, who naturally told her husband, Tess's peppery Greek father. His reaction . . . "If you are married, you must live together!" . . . was no doubt what Horace had had in mind all along.

The newlyweds had just one short year . . . eleven months, to be exact . . . to enjoy being a twosome. I muscled in on them the following January 17. The family joke through the years was, I was born in January, and they were married in February. Today that wouldn't be considered unusual . . . let alone funny.

To their credit . . . intruder or not . . . they made me most welcome.

On Marriage

After all the wedding dust has settled comes the marriage . . . But somewhere in between is the inevitable period of adjustment . . . to each other . . . to life together.

We hear, from time to time, an expression that is one of the nicest compliments a husband or wife can pay one another . . . "This is my best friend."

If a marriage works, it means that two people have found a way to make most, if not all, ingredients blend. The list of things to cope with is longer than it seemed at

first blush, when you entered into the contract . . .
love, children, in-laws, sex, money, job pressures, habits,
moods, basic differences, and so on, ad infinitum.
Whether it is some or all of the above . . . to handle any
of it, you had jolly well *better* be best friends, or forget it.
It doesn't happen right away . . . it's something to
grow into . . . otherwise, the whole arrangement
comes apart at the seams. I learned the difference
through experience. I am not proud of the fact that,
years ago, I didn't stick around long enough to reach that
point.

Everyone is a self-styled expert on why "Those two
will never make it!" . . . or "They were made for each
other!" . . . "What does he (she) see in her (him)?" is
another good one.

In truth, not a soul, outside of the two people involved
. . . not children, parents, or friends . . . *no one* has the
foggiest notion of what goes on between a husband and a
wife.

Even with close friends you think you know so well,
there are some surprises. Two people, both of whom I
love very deeply, seemed to be the ultimate match. Both
are intelligent, beautiful, and brilliant in their own fields
. . . Mary Tyler Moore and Grant Tinker. Such perfect
casting *must* work . . . and it did for seventeen years.
Today they are still intelligent, beautiful, and successful,
and have fully established lives . . . but with two other
people. Nice ones, I might add.

In a breakup like that, too often, one or the other of
your beloved friends is lost to you. Typically of both

Grant and Mary, however . . . no situation was ever allowed to develop that would make taking sides, or choosing between them, necessary. As it turns out, I now have four friends . . . and though Mary and Grant's marriage is no longer . . . the *friendship* between them is intact.

The judge who performed the wedding ceremony for Mary and Grant in 1962 did the same for Allen and me a year later. The knot he tied for the Tinkers may have slipped, but the one for the Luddens kept getting tighter. It took cancer to pull it apart.

By now you may have gathered that I was a rather reluctant bride . . . fool that I was. Consequently, the settling in process may have taken me somewhat longer than is the norm.

When we returned to New York from our abbreviated honeymoon, we went directly from the airport to the CBS studio to tape "Password." Playing it a little close, wouldn't you say?

With the bridegroom moderating, of course . . . Jack Paar was booked on the show to play the game opposite the bride . . . me. It was his wedding gift to us, as he would never do game shows as a rule.

And then, at long last, the time came to go home . . . to Briarcliff Manor up in Westchester County. We didn't find our Chappaqua house until two weeks later.

When we arrived, we walked in, to find the house filled with posters and streamers and balloons . . . all proclaiming WELCOME HOME! and CONGRATULATIONS! All three kids were home, and there was a lot of shrieking and hugging and kissing and giggling . . . as well as much barking from Willie and Emma, who were quick to get into the spirit of the thing. I shall never forget how much that warm welcome from everybody meant, and how it helped me over the first hurdle . . . I will be ever-grateful.

That first hurdle was . . . the fact that this was the house Allen and Margaret had moved into, just before she went to the hospital for the last time. He had, subsequently, had it all redecorated . . . but the beautiful new kitchen had been started before she had gone.

I had known all this, going in . . . and had convinced myself that I could handle it. We even walked through the house that first week, with a builder friend, talking about some further remodeling.

Fate stepped in, on cue, to help solve what I was beginning to realize could become a very real private problem. Our friends the O'Briens stopped by one morning, all excited, to tell us about a lovely old farmhouse on five and a half acres that had just come up for sale in Chappaqua . . . which was only a couple of villages to the north.

We went to look at it that very afternoon. By evening, it was ours. It really was beautiful, and . . . thank God . . . everyone in the family loved it.

With all the adjustments I knew *I* was making, I never kidded myself into believing that the other members of the family weren't making even bigger ones. I kept wondering if they were thinking of Margaret . . . Well, of *course* they were thinking of Margaret . . . I guess I meant comparing. I felt a little like Mrs. DeWinter in

Rebecca, except that Margaret had been a wonderful lady. And I knew she would forever remain that wonderful forty-seven-year-old lady . . . no matter how the world moved on for the rest of us.

I made dumb mistakes.

I carved a pumpkin to surprise everybody for Halloween . . . and was puzzled by the lack of enthusiasm it received . . . from a normally exuberant family. Allen had to explain that it was on Halloween that Margaret died.

Beautiful as our new home was, I was bombarded by private attacks of homesickness that would strike with such a vengeance, it was actual physical pain. Impossible to explain to anybody . . . even now. I had the world on a string . . . what more could I ask?

My folks came to visit the first of November . . . and they fell in love with the whole area. They were already in love with Allen.

At the end of the visit, when we drove them to the airport, Dad was showing signs of a slight cold. The doctor popped him into the hospital for a few days when he got back to California. Not to worry . . . they sent him home again the following Saturday morning. That afternoon his heart stopped.

I flew out on one plane, Allen followed on another as soon as he got off the air. Allen had to go back right after the funeral, but insisted that I stay on for a couple of days, to pack Mom up and bring her home to us for a little while.

It was when I called the Los Angeles *Times* the following Friday morning, to cancel her paper, that a shaking
voice on the phone informed me that John Kennedy had
just been shot!

Mom and I arrived back in Chappaqua . . . where for
the entire weekend we all clung to each other . . .
locked to the television set, mourning with the rest of the
nation, as we watched the presidential funeral ceremo-
nies. President Kennedy's death, and my father's are
forever inseparable in my mind.

At some point during that timeless weekend, I came to
realize how much it meant to have Allen there . . . beside me, sharing the grief we felt for both men . . . and
from that moment I began to think of us as a unit, rather
than two separate entities.

For the rest of our time together, once I finally saw the
light, all of our problems came from the outside . . .
never between the two of us. And we handled those
problems *together*. I'm not for one minute saying it was
smooth sailing from then on in . . . but I no longer had
my foot out the door. I finally began to know what marriage was really about.

Close as I was to my mother and dad . . . I could
never really understand how . . . or why . . . their
marriage seemed to work.

In all those years, they never seemed to settle into that
placid, taking-each-other-for-granted existence that I
saw in other families. (Keep in mind, Betty, you were
seeing those families from the outside. What did we say
about "No one ever knows"?)

My parents were terribly in love . . . and, on occasion, it would be just that . . . *terribly* in love. An "I can't live with you, can't live without you" relationship.

They actually did split up . . . briefly . . . twice. But I wasn't the first in our family to marry a dynamite salesman . . . there was no way Dad was going to lose her.

Both Tess and Horace adored their only child . . . yet, at no time, did I ever get an inkling that they were staying together because of me. They couldn't stay apart.

They would try so hard not to quarrel where I could hear . . . but it's difficult in a small tuned-in family not to know when something is going on. Mom would flare, Dad's lip would tighten . . . maybe even stay that way for a day or two . . . during which they would be elaborately polite to each other. Sooner or later, the sun would come back out, and the fun would return.

At this late date, there is no reason to bother you with trying to figure out two people you don't even know. Personally, however, I find it fascinating to realize that the two people I loved so well, and believed I knew completely . . . had a side, together, that I really didn't know at all.

That's a facet of marriage as well. To be sure.

On Widowhood

What happens afterward? When a marriage has been terminated . . . not by anyone's decision, but by something even more irrevocable . . . where do you go from here?

    It varies from individual to individual, as with anything else . . . but there are certain areas of common ground. Like the recurring question . . . from personal friends, newly widowed, or in letters from viewers, or, now and then, in talking to myself . . . "Does it *ever* get any better?"

    Sure it does. If not better . . . let's say it gets *different.*

    At times, one gets the feeling that the whole world is full of nothing but widows. The actuarial tables are way ahead of me, I know . . . there are a lot of us around. But let's look at it this way . . . at least we have more going for us today, perhaps, than at any other point in time. There are some fairly viable alternative choices, if we are forced to go it alone. Small comfort, I know, if you are in terrible pain at this moment . . . but something to keep in the back of your mind when strength begins to seep back in.

    To draw differences in situations, once again I have to resort to the personal. I have no other yardstick.

It is obvious that the small White family was pretty sufficient unto itself . . . to a fault. There were friends around the perimeter, but social activity was minimal. My father's daily work furnished him with all the outside people contact he really wanted. I had school friends, early on, then entered a work situation that was nothing but people. This meant that my mother was left with the at home challenge of keeping our rather parochial life-style interesting. She did a bang-up job.

Our pets have always been dealt in as equal members of our household . . . which should come as no surprise. Prior to the time I made my big decision to move east with Allen, I had been back living at home with my folks for quite some time. Able to come and go on my frequent trips out of town, it was not only a pleasant situation, but it meant the dogs could all stay together . . . cared for by the world's best baby-sitters.

So it was, then, that in early 1963, Mom's family consisted of Dad, Betty, Bandit (my fifteen year-old Pekingese who died shortly before I left), Dancer (a twelve-year-old poodle), and Stormy, (a St. Bernard, ten). Within less than a year, I had left and Dad had died, as had all three of the dogs.

All Mom had in the way of *close* friends or family in California were her brother Tom (my pal) and his wife Dale. We didn't know it then, but he only had two years left, himself.

We brought Mom back to us when Dad died in November . . . but right after Christmas, she felt she had to get on with her life, and returned to California.

But where to begin?

She sold the house and moved into an apartment . . . which at first only served to accentuate the aloneness.

One day, when I had said, once too often, that I wished she had friends to help, she said, "What do I do? Do I walk up on the street and say, 'Be my friend!'?" It was a cry from the heart . . . and we reminded her of it many times, later on.

My mother had worked as a bookkeeper before she was married, but not since. She was one of the fortunate ones who had been left enough money to live on. Determined not to sit and vegetate, she began to do volunteer work . . . first at the hospital at U.C.L.A. She did a little bit of everything, and everything she did won her new and lasting friends. Her first close pal was head of volunteers at the hospital at that time, Ruth Murch. It was not too long after that that Mom was helping Rufus through her own challenge of losing her husband. For me, Ruth is still my Udder Mudder.

She was invited . . . no, commandeered into the Motion Picture Mothers, a hard-working group of ladies whose kids happen to be in show biz . . . and through their efforts they raise a *lot* of money for the Motion Picture Country Home and Hospital. Together, Mom and DeDe Ball, Lucy's mother, joined the group, although both were anything but "joiners." It was sort of on an "I will if you will" basis. Mom always said it was the best move she ever made . . . how she loved working, and laughing, with that gang.

Before our astonished eyes, it wasn't too long before our "nonjoiner" was elected recording secretary . . . and saying no thank you when they talked about her as

president. My friendless little mother had blossomed
into a mistress of revels, and her calendar was full!

We noticed that her circle of friends consisted primar-
ily of other women . . . widows mostly, and a few cou-
ples . . . she was not interested in finding another man.
In fact, she got downright testy when someone would try
and set up something. For the record, with a face and
legs like hers . . . that choice was her own.

Allen was as proud of her as I was . . . he'd tease her
with, "What have you been doing, Tess . . . stopping
people on the street again to make friends?"

As close as Tess and I were . . . and there were those
who thought we were the same person . . . our lives as
widows differ entirely. Understandably.

My line of work has always meant dealing with people
on all sides, constantly. Dear friends have been around,
and still are today . . . the problem was lack of time to
do them justice. This was not only because of work com-
mitments, much of it was my own doing. I enjoyed
spending a lot of the time I had with my mother. She was
still more fun than most . . . interesting and interested
. . . a great buddy with whom I could talk in shorthand,
without having to *explain*.

When I used to hear myself going on about how I
enjoyed being alone . . . I always secretly wondered if
that would still be the case when the day came when I
really *was* alone. I am most grateful to say . . . it is. To
all of those who worried that my "mother complex"
would result in emotional disaster when I lost her, be of
good cheer. I miss her at every turn, certainly . . . but

we had such quality time together that I don't have to use up the strength she left me with, on any guilts or "if onlys." I still enjoy her.

As a widow . . . unlike Tess, suddenly cut adrift and having to build a busy schedule from scratch . . . my situation has been just the opposite. Believe me, I *never* take that for granted. *I appreciate how fortunate I am!* But I still fight for and treasure those times when I can close the door and be all by myself, to recharge the battery . . . (pets, of course, are exempt) . . . and I find myself saying no to things, perhaps more than I should. Except work. So while there *is* a lot of Tess in me . . . there is more Horace than I'd ever imagined.

It is fascinating to see how our lives manage to sort themselves out and regenerate, if we let them. My mother had another completely different life for the twenty-two years after Dad died . . . and a full and happy one, despite the dismal beginning.

Allen had another whole unit of his life after he lost Margaret . . . yet, at the time, he would never have believed such a thing possible. His love for me in no way encroached on what he had had with her.

For me, after Allen left, my work shifted into another, more accelerated gear, and life gets more interesting with every day that passes. My animal work continues, as well as some charity appearances . . . and, best of all . . . there are some great Superfriends to glue it all together. They understand my alone times . . . and I have the comfort of knowing they are *there.* How I *wish* everyone had that luxury.

Widows have another alternative we haven't talked about. What about an arrangement similar to that of the Golden Girls?

Although Blanche and Dorothy and Sophia and Rose are together more for companionship than economy, the sharing could make sense from either standpoint. I have received quite a few letters applauding the concept as a great possibility. I have yet to hear from anyone so far saying, "We tried it, and the idea's a bummer!"

You already know how I value solitude, so my advice must not be taken too seriously. All I *would* suggest, however, is that you think twice before risking a Super-friend on the experiment . . . maybe you should try it out with someone you can afford to lose. Remember, the Golden Girls only live together for half an hour at a time . . . once a week.

On Love

Ask three people to give their definition of love, and you'll get nine answers. At least.

"Love" covers almost anything. Love is what you feel for your family, your parents, your friends . . . two-legged and four. Or you can add to the list . . . one loves his car, music, chocolate, his favorite comedian, the Dodgers . . .

We have addressed some of these elsewhere here (not

the Dodgers) so let's narrow it down to the man/woman relationship. Narrow it down, she says! Love still covers such a lot of territory. There are so many different kinds and degrees of love, and they all weave into the same fabric . . . the more varied the threads, the more interesting the tapestry . . . you.

Love can be pleasure, or pain . . . sometimes even therapy.

At one point in my life I drifted into a romantic encounter that had absolutely nowhere to go. However, for a time it made life a very warm and tender adventure. No, it was no one you would know, so don't bother to guess.

It happened when . . . and no doubt *because* . . . I was at my most vulnerable. I shall be eternally grateful for a lovely memory, and there was no damage done . . . it could have been a lot worse. Instead, it served an invaluable purpose . . . I felt like a person again . . . and, for the first time in a long time, an attractive one. It isn't *what* it was, but rather *that* it was. It may have saved my life at the time.

Love is a matter of personal semantics. Elizabeth Taylor has often been quoted as saying she was only happy when she was in love. "In love" is such a special state . . . again, my own personal interpretation . . . that it happens but rarely in a lifetime. More than once, but certainly not often. And for me, it isn't an annual bloomer . . . for one season only. With the right care and attention, it's a hardy perennial.

Let me paraphrase Elizabeth. I am probably happiest when I'm "in like." You know the feeling . . . when someone has caught your attention, but good, even though they might not be aware of it. When the mere sound of his name can give you a little private buzz. When you find yourself replaying things he has said, in the back of your mind . . . or quoting him inordinately, whether it fits into the conversation or not. "In like" is a grown-up (!?) equivalent of "crush," I guess. It is that lovely *before* state of mind when there are not yet any problems or choices. It is fleeting. It doesn't stand still. It must grow into something more serious, or evaporate completely, leaving only a slight momentary disappointment.

Now . . . should that private buzz change to a constant roar . . . if he never leaves the back of your mind for an instant, and you alternate between a state of euphoria and sheer panic . . . that, dear reader, is a sure sign that you are what I call in "fatuation." Maintaining any kind of perspective at this juncture is a lost cause . . . you just have to steer the boat the best you can. Difficulties are compounded when you find you don't recognize yourself as the same sane person you've always lived in. Bad decisions and misjudgments abound . . . but there are goodies as well, make no mistake. When it is over, just hope you emerge wiser, and relatively unscathed.

But then . . .

Rarely . . . oh, so rarely . . . the feeling simply will not go away. Instead, a deep warning bell begins to sound. Whether or not you are ready to listen, it says, "This is different." Try as you will to silence it, bury it, abuse it, laugh at it, or run from it . . . you can't deny it.

You are "In Love." And nothing is ever quite the same again.

Incurably romantic? Maybe not.

Fairy tales and Barbara Cartland novels notwithstanding, we know that over a lifetime it is possible to have more than one deep and abiding love. There have even been cases on record where someone was genuinely and totally in love with two people at the same time. Knowing my problem with decisions, I don't even want to contemplate the inherent difficulties in that situation.

How do you *know* when what you feel for someone is beyond "in like" or in "fatuation"? I don't think you do, at first . . . for a short while they all seem to have the same symptoms . . . more . . . or less. Time has a way of sorting the wheat from the chaff, and before long the day might arrive when you think, "What did I ever *see* in him!"

Unhappily, if time takes too long with its sorting, a lot of mistakes can be made in the interim.

What if the feeling stands the test of time, and qualifies as pure gold . . . not brass . . . this time around? And let's say the feeling is mutual, not a one-sided affair. That should be the end of the rainbow, shouldn't it? . . . They lived happily ever after.

You and I know it doesn't work that way. People change, situations change, problems prove insurmountable . . . and lives go in different directions. But that does not mean that the love wasn't very special for its time. It has earned its own little private place within you forever. You may even polish it now and then.

Sometimes . . . often . . . when the love has been

that strong, it evolves into a lasting, warm friendship. It may have to undergo an uncomfortable period of adjustment, but once out of the storm, it can be a tranquil and unbreakable relationship . . . with a set of memories all its own.

Even discussing love raises more questions than it answers. If they haven't been able to figure it out in thousands of years, I seriously doubt if we will here.

What I do know for sure about any and all love is that it *can* die from neglect, or abuse. That you have to work at it to enjoy it. And that I never want to be without it.

On Grief . . . and Hope

Grief is not a real fun subject. There are few laughs to be had here, so you are welcome to skip to the next section. I will understand completely.

Inevitably, grief does find its way to each of us at some time or other. How we handle it, or how long we let it stay, is something we can't predict ahead of time. It is such a totally personal experience . . . it seems to cut all the circuits, temporarily, and insulate you against sympathy, condolences, comfort . . . anything that might diminish it. Numbness alternates with searing pain, and each individual must find his own way of getting through it. Talk about on-the-job training.

Allen's and my relationship was on so many levels *beyond* husband/friend. He would keep a pragmatic anchor on some of my flightier ideas . . . he would critique my performance on camera . . . he even kept a watchful eye on how my makeup or hair looked. He would be tickled when I got what he called "the writing look," and I never felt I had completed anything until I gave it to him to read. As well as a great kisser, he was a good, tough editor. Oh, how I need him now.

For a lifetime, my mother served as my mentor, and my best audience . . . but also my severest critic. She didn't pussyfoot around if she didn't like something . . . she had a good eye and I listened. Again, it may sound as though I had no mind of my own . . . believe me, I did, and I would go down swinging if I disagreed with either of their opinions.

With Allen gone, I still had Tess . . . but only for a little while. More and more, as she got weaker, our roles began to reverse. I almost became the mother . . . she the child I adored . . . and then, she just wasn't there anymore.

One of the toughest things for me to handle, among many, was the sudden realization that I was in charge. No longer was there someone to turn to and ask an opinion, or a decision . . . even a painful criticism. Being the new boss, you are aware that you are expected to do something, but haven't a clue as to what it should be . . . and even if you *knew* what it was, there's no time to do it because of so many maddening details and the paperwork that must be dealt with constantly. It took me a while to get wise to the fact that those very details were

what kept me going forward . . . they wouldn't wait
while I jumped into bed and pulled the covers over my
head. They kept me occupied through the first few
hours, days, weeks . . . until I began to breathe again.

Grief, the monster, doesn't just finally go away. It goes
into a very light sleep, deep inside you, where, now and
then, something unexpected will cause it to stir uneasily.
You tread very lightly until it dozes off again.

I have talked a great deal in these pages about missing
the people I love. Deliver me from becoming one of
those who wear their grief like a mantle . . . almost
seeming to grow to enjoy it . . . using it to justify anything and everything. They feed on it constantly, keeping
it very much awake and alive. It becomes too easy to stay
on that long downward spiral, until getting back to anything near a normal life is next to impossible without a
great deal of outside help. It follows that those around
them aren't having any real picnic either.

The Greeks had a word for it . . . Pythagoras said a
long long time ago, "If you have a wounded heart, touch
it as little as you would a wounded eye . . . There are
only two remedies for the suffering of the soul: hope and
patience."

It is impossible to talk about grief without also talking
about hope . . . without some degree of hope, grief
doesn't bear discussing.

It is a constant source of amazement to me to think
back on the number of times in my life when things were

at their bleakest . . . when I thought there was absolutely no hope of anything ever being worthwhile again.

Superfriends don't like it when you talk about them too much . . . that isn't what the friendship is about. And that privacy is one of the special things you love about them.

But I am going to make two exceptions . . . because they make the point of hope so eloquently.

Mary Tyler Moore Levine and I don't see each other often . . . we live a continent apart. If we're lucky, we may be together once a year . . . we talk on the phone for a minute maybe every few months . . . but she has been my strength more times than she will ever know.

In the middle of the night . . . one terrible night . . . at the hospital in Monterey, California, Allen was in a coma and not expected to make it to daylight. Mary's son Richie had died that day, and she had just flown in from New York to Los Angeles. It was around midnight when she called me . . . I took the call at the nurse's station . . . and I can still hear her say, "Oh, Betty . . . where did it all go wrong for us?" We cried at each other for maybe ten minutes, holding so close.

When I went back into Allen's room . . . for the first time I was able to let it all go. The purge was painful, but, oh, so necessary. In her grief, Mary had helped me. We both came through the black time, somehow.

Mary had a lot more heartache ahead of her . . . so did I. But today, we're not only "still here," as the song goes . . . we are both tremendously happy and healthy and productive . . . with completely new lives. You could never have made either one of us believe such a thing was possible that miserable night in Monterey.

At that time, Mary and Grant had long since gone their separate ways, but, as usual Grant was there for both Mary and me during that nightmare period.

When Allen's doctors said he could be brought back to Los Angeles after three weeks in the Monterey Community Hospital . . . it was Grant who sent the ambulance plane to transport him.

During Allen's last week . . . although it was supposed to be NO VISITORS . . . it was Grant who showed up every afternoon . . . saying he just happened to be in the neighborhood. (His office was fifteen miles away.)

One early morning I had to tell Grant that the battle was over . . . he and Melanie came and spent the afternoon with me.

And when I asked if he would mind saying a few words at the service . . . Grant simply said, "You don't worry about that. You let me produce it." And what a lovely send-off he put together for his best best friend.

It was not until weeks later when the news was made public . . . that I found out what else had happened on the day Allen died. Grant had been offered and had accepted the position of Chairman of the Board of NBC . . . at a luncheon meeting on *that day*. His career . . . his whole *life* had undergone a monumental change . . . yet he and Melanie were with me that afternoon for a warm, unhurried visit as though there was nothing else going on in the world.

Among other things, Allen had great taste in best best friends.

When I count the high spots that have taken place in my life since that grim time, I determine never to give up again. That is, of course, until the next black time, when,

once more, I will be certain that things are absolutely
hopeless.

Will I ever learn?

Where did Emily Dickinson get off being so wise?

> "Hope is the thing with feathers
>   That perches in the soul,
>   It sings the tune without the words,
>   And never stops at all."

VI

BRINGING UP
THE REAR

On Forward

This book is due in the publisher's hands this coming Thursday. I feel like I'm turning in a term paper, except that this has been much more fun. If you have hung in there with me to this point . . . many thanks.

Before I bail out . . . two things have happened in the last five days that somehow brought everything into focus for me.

The first one was last Wednesday night . . . when I learned that you can't trust anybody.

Following rehearsal, Bea, Rue, Estelle, and I were scheduled to do a photo layout for McCall's magazine. We were all grousing about having to go through the long makeup and hair session on a day when we weren't taping . . . it takes over an hour . . . and then get gussied up in fancy wardrobe, after rehearsing all day. Our photographer, Wayne Williams, promised to keep it as short as possible . . . and we all started horsing around while he snapped pictures.

Suddenly . . . out of nowhere . . . Ralph Edwards materialized, with That Book under his arm . . . and announced, "This Is Your Life, Betty White!"

There is no way to describe the next few hours. First, the sheer panic, when I literally considered running away . . . followed by total catatonic shock.

We've all seen Ralph confound people through the years . . . 504 times, if you're counting . . . but never,

repeat *never* do you think it can happen to you. *You* would
be too observant and aware not to suspect that *something*
was going on . . . especially when so many people were
in on the secret . . . The girls knew, the director, the
producers, my trusted secretary, Gail, who helped Ralph
sort it out, my housekeeper . . . and God only knows
who else. Well, maybe *you* would be too observant and
aware to be fooled, but not this kid.

At this point, Bea and Rue and Estelle could laugh with
relief, take off their finery, and go home . . . the subter-
fuge was over. (In all truth, you can't imagine what a test
of friendship it was for them to go through all that phony
preparation . . . which they hate at the best of times. I
am eternally grateful!)

But for me it was just beginning. From here on in,
everything was out of my hands. Ralph transported me
to the Aquarius Theater. Someone else took my car keys.
Someone brought my street clothes from my dressing
room. Another elf brought my car to the theater.

I kept worrying because I had dinner plans with my
friend Rudy Behlmer and didn't know how to reach him
to cancel. I needn't have worried . . . there he was at
the theater when we arrived . . . he'd been a co-con-
spirator since the beginning! *Nobody* is to be trusted.

One of the reasons . . . or at least my excuse . . .
that I had been taken in so completely, was that "This Is
Your Life" had been off the air for a while, and I had no
idea they were planning a special.

All that was going through my mind while waiting for
Ralph to lead me onstage was "Who will they get to come

on . . . everybody I know is dead!" Another hazard
that fretted me was my rotten memory.

Well . . . Ralph had done a superb job in the surprise
department:

My Beverly Hills High School drama teacher, Robert
Whitten.

Also from Beverly High, my first leading man! Larry
Rose and I had done *Pride and Prejudice,* our senior play
. . . and they brought him in from Washington, D.C.
. . . still in costume!

Jack Paar flew in from New York!

Mark Goodson flew in from New York!

Gene Rayburn flew in from New York!

The whole gang from "The Mary Tyler Moore Show"
were there . . . Ed Asner, Valerie Harper, Gavin Mac-
Leod, Georgia Engel, Cloris Leachman . . . and somehow Ted Knight was there, I swear.

Then, *live* by satellite from New York, there was Mary
herself! She's in the middle of a Broadway show, *Sweet
Sue,* or she would have been there in person. As it was,
she and my buddy Dash, her golden retriever, introduced me to her new basset griffon puppy, Dudley!

And then Johnny Grant, the mayor of Hollywood, presented perhaps the best surprise of all. There is to be a
new star on the Hollywood Walk of Fame . . . for Allen
Ludden! Oh, would that tickle him!

As if I wasn't wiped out by now, in walks Grant Tinker
to tell me that Allen's star will be placed on Hollywood
Boulevard right next to mine . . . (put there years ago).
That tore it.

More friends were there . . . Don Fedderson, who
started my career when he put me on his station in "The

Al Jarvis Show," then later, with George Tibbles we partnered on "Life with Elizabeth."

Talented, funny, music man Frank DeVol, who had been my musical director and right hand on the daytime variety series we did.

From another major part of my life, the Morris Animal Foundation, executive director Claude Ramsey, flown in from Denver, and our president, Dona Singlehurst, in from Hawaii.

If anyone ever wonders whether "This Is Your Life" is on the level . . . or asks if they really do surprise people . . . check with me. For the record, I learned that if a subject should ever find out before the show, the mission is scrubbed, and they start over with someone else. Even after all that preparation and meticulous detail . . . and money! Only on a couple of occasions was the surprise blown, when they were so close to airtime they couldn't abort . . . so it was explained at the top of the show that the subject had found out inadvertently . . . while it was no longer a surprise, they would carry on with the party. Only a couple of slip-ups, out of 504 chances!! Ralph should be running the CIA.

You may have gathered by now that it was a night I shall never forget.

And the other thing that happened in the last five days: This morning, I did a radio commercial with George Burns. We've been friends for a long time, but I've never worked with him before. At ten A.M. sharp, this dapper ninety-one-year-old charmer came in to the recording studio, greeted me, and we proceeded to read the script without rehearsal. One take, and George said, lighting his cigar, "We're never going to get any better than that. Next!"

We are going to do the TV version of the same commercial next month, and we've had a tough time setting a date for it because the schedule is so crowded. Not mine . . . *his!*

In the writing of these pieces, I have spent a lot of time looking back. The timing of "This Is Your Life" couldn't have been more appropriate . . . it was like the capper.

On the other hand, seeing George this morning, and listening to him, it became abundantly clear . . . the reason he is so full of it is that he keeps planning ahead. He looks forward to the things he *will* be doing . . . his movies, his nightclub act . . . which in no way detracts from his fondness for where he's *been.* He is booked solid till after his hundredth birthday!

So . . . I have thoroughly enjoyed putting this exercise in retrospection down on paper . . . and "This Is Your Life" was a wonderful sentimental journey.

Now, however, I'm with George.

Next?

Afterword

As promised, this has simply been a collection of random thoughts on how I feel on a variety of subjects . . . about the things that work for me, and the things that don't.

It has been fun to do. I feel a little like the psychiatrist who, after making passionate love to his patient, says, "Well, that solves my problem. What's yours?"

I have but one nagging little doubt. It does sound a bit like *Golden Rules*, doesn't it? Dear Gussie! Back to the drawing board!